Rockefeller's Follies

Rockefeller's

AN UNAUTHORIZED

Follies

VIEW OF NELSON A. ROCKEFELLER

BY WILLIAM RODGERS

STEIN AND DAY/*Publishers*/*New York*

Designed by David Miller
Printed in the United States of America
Published simultaneously in Canada by Saunders of Toronto, Ltd.

Stein and Day/*Publishers*/7 East 48 Street, New York, N.Y. 10017

TO *Katie* AND *Ange*

ACKNOWLEDGMENTS

I am grateful to the many men and women, in and out of government, who gave me so much of their time to talk with me, to provide information, and to express their views. It is quite clear that thoughtful people see value in dissent, dialogue, and communication, even if they do not always care to expose their own positions to public scrutiny; none who talked with me in trust is betrayed here.

This book is offered as a contribution to open and rational political dialogue, and to an electorate which is too often managed, muted, and misinformed.

I acknowledge, and express my thanks for, the assistance and counsel of people on the editorial staffs of *Patent Trader,* Mount Kisco, New York; *The Independent Herald,* Harrison, New York, and the Gannett-owned Westchester-Rockland Newspapers, Inc., as well as to librarians in a number of Hudson Valley communities.

I am especially appreciative for the help of Mr. Rod Vandivert, Executive Director of the Scenic Hudson Preservation Conference; of a number of legislators in Washington and Albany; and of Mr. Merrill Folsom, chief of *The New York Times* Bureau at White Plains, New York. Any interpretations, or errors, if any, in this work are, of course, mine—not theirs.

WILLIAM RODGERS

Arch Hill
Briarcliff Manor, N.Y.
May, 1966

CONTENTS

Rockefeller's Follies

The Two-dimensional Billionaire

In most of the literature written about Nelson Aldrich Rockefeller, Governor of New York State and dominant member of a family of third-generation billionaires, there is a hollow echo of unbelievability.

The sequence of events is duly reported, the dates on which he began and terminated various ventures and jobs are listed, his ringing and declarative assertions are quoted, his objectives are cited and reviewed, his motives clarified in rational and uncompromisingly favorable terms. Like a good man in a Victorian novel, he emerges from a shelf of biographical material as a two-dimensional character intended to set an example for people wavering in their determination to do right at all times.

Although Mr. Rockefeller and his staff of imagemakers are more or less responsible for the well laundered biographical versions of his life, the various publications are nonetheless unfair to him. He is a more complete personality than the literature about him reflects since, like the rest of us, he is composed of human ingredients that are deleted from the posed portraits drawn by professional chroniclers.

Published assessments of Nelson Rockefeller have generally suffered from an overemphasis on public relations which, in company with enormous wealth, helped fashion the latter-day public image of Nelson's grandfather, John D. Rockefeller, Sr., and sustains the family's public posture to this day.

Surrounding Nelson the man, the Governor, the figure of wealth and personal power, and the occasional jovial man-of-the-people who expresses a warm affection for everybody, is a staff of highly paid individuals whose duties are both compartmentalized and varied. These carefully screened people are for the most part the very soul of courtesy. They are a careful representation of races and ethnic groups, and they include men and women from the upper social strata, from the great American middle class, and individuals who are triumphs, in terms of education and development, over early poverty in lower class origins.

But in the Rockefeller world there exists a rigid, iron-fisted code enforced with a multiplicity of velvet gloves. It centers on "an inviolate taboo on all publicity regarding the private lives of the Rockefeller brothers and their families." *

In practice, the taboo extends beyond the private lives of the Rockefellers, who are perhaps the richest family on earth. In the case of Nelson Rockefeller, the taboo protects, distorts, and cuts off critical assessment of important aspects of his public life as well. By virtue of the enforcement of an inner-circle doctrine, harnessed to the corporate family image handed down to the present generations of Rockefellers, Nelson—perhaps more than his brothers—has become a kind of institutionalized man, valued and despised for the power he wields and represents; courted, used, and sometimes abused in the manner

* The quotation is from the book, *The Real Rockefeller,* by Frank Gervasi, a campaign biography published by Atheneum, New York, in 1964.

14

of a bank or giant corporation, whose operations offend, injure, please, and enrich in turn.

A corporation runs his household, buys and sells and operates his land; the corporate style is reflected in his New York offices. All about him is an atmosphere of hush, efficiency, impersonal detachment, and security that are the characteristics not so much of an individual as of a company; a contrived, tasteful, and coolly planned operation behind which the man himself is shielded from confrontation with the irritations common to ordinary life, and from the sights, sounds, and smells that aggravate all but the extraordinarily well endowed, or the neurotically secluded, in a frenzied, fast-paced, and anxiety-ridden urban world.

Such protection and environment are afforded many men of wealth, men whose managerial talents or special skills for making money give them privileges normally beyond purchasable price. Yet Nelson Rockefeller is a very special case. A protective wall has long stood between the urban world and the extensive, organized institution which orbits around this energetic, even kinetic, oddly driven man who constitutes an outsized central core in a galaxy of carefully positioned satellites.

In common with nearly all very wealthy people, Nelson Rockefeller purchases with his resources a life of order, privacy when it is desired, a controlled and serene environment in which to work or wander, reflect or play. He acquires works of art and treasures of both transient and lasting value, and sometimes even participates in the decision-making processes which determine what part of his enormous resources shall be deflected to philanthropy, to causes of interest and speculation. With masterful poise, he often seems at ease in the most raucous environment— such as the halls of the legislature—endowed with vitality and virility, expressed calmly and exuberantly by turn,

15

with an exultant charm that he appears to be able to turn on and off like a current responsive to his will.

Yet he can be sour and surly, moody and unpredictable, puzzling, chill, and unresponsive. "He has," in the words of one observer who has known him casually for years, "a talent for offending his friends and supporting their foes."

A rich man, it is said, is only a poor man with money. F. Scott Fitzgerald was fascinated by, and made his literary home among, the wealthy; he wrote that the "very rich" were different from other people. Whether or not Fitzgerald's comment is applicable to Nelson Rockefeller, his life in politics makes it possible to assess him—and his record—on the basis of his public conduct. The protective wall can no longer altogether conceal the full dimension of the man. We find that he is rather an ordinary man, capable of folly, cupidity, deception, and self-delusion, as well as acts of generosity and humanity.

If a man can be assessed and judged by the way he uses power, what that power is used to achieve, how he responds in frustration, defeat, and victory, what he believes in and fights for, then we have at hand sufficient material to appraise the man who would most certainly have been President of the United States if he had had Richard Nixon's opportunity against John F. Kennedy.

Nelson was born in 1908, one of a family of six children—five boys and a girl. Educated by tutors until he was ten, he entered Manhattan's Lincoln School at 646 Park Avenue, a private institution supported in part by family funds and used as a kind of teaching laboratory by Columbia University Teachers College to experiment with the progressive educational concepts of John Dewey. All of the Rockefellers except the oldest, John D., III (who

16

went to Browning School), attended Lincoln, which relocated in 1920 uptown off Amsterdam Avenue. Until the school moved, the boys often walked from the family house on West 54th Street, just off Fifth Avenue, and sometimes, it is reported in biographical sketches written by others, they went on roller skates. A former teacher at Lincoln, however, has remembered seeing the boys pull up to the school door in the family's black limousine.

In this demanding if permissive school, Nelson is said to have flourished. He was popular both with his companions and his teachers, although the latter acknowledged that his academic progress was not overly satisfactory. He seems to have demonstrated in his early teens a capacity for taking charge of things, a characteristic sometimes described as cocky but more often seen as an indication of developing leadership.

His hopes of going to Princeton University were dashed by the specter that haunts so many thousands of college-bound students today: his grades weren't good enough, although in his last two years at Lincoln his academic standing, in response to disciplinary directions from his father, John D. Rockefeller, Jr., had steadily improved. At eighteen, he entered Dartmouth College. Here, he had trouble with his grades until his junior year. Then, under the influence of his close friend and roommate, John French, Jr., he began to show real academic progress. John French was one of Dartmouth's brighter young men. Nelson called him "brilliant" and has said that his friend had a "tremendous influence" on him. Both young men had been critical of fraternities and in their sophomore year are reported to have written an article citing Greek Letter societies as snobbish and undemocratic. Subsequently they both joined Psi Upsilon, but did not move into the fraternity house. In their last year they lived in the Senior House of the Casque and Gauntlet. In his final two years at Dartmouth, Nelson put an increasing amount of time into his studies, finishing his junior year in the top 3 per cent of his class. He made Phi Beta Kappa and was graduated *cum laude*. Like many boys with older and brighter brothers, Nelson was a late bloomer, and his concerned but loving parents needn't have worried about him at all.

Nelson earned an A in economics for his honors thesis, a lengthy paper that disclosed a thoughtful concern about the origins of the Rockefeller family fortune. While the thesis reflected none of the criticism contained in Ida Tarbell's classic muckraking book, which much earlier had excoriated the ruthless and lucrative creation of the oil monopoly by John D. Rockefeller, Sr., it did raise questions about his grandfather's monopolistic practices and, by extension, revealed a rather touching sensitivity to the long sustained and harsh judgment in which millions of people all over the world held the titan of the oil industry and his heirs.

It is altogether probable that the young man was perturbed by guilt over the business conduct of his aging grandfather. Blameless as the grandchildren were for the accomplishments and unsavory reputation of John D. Rockefeller, Sr., throughout the world, it would have been impossible at that time for Nelson to reflect on the family wealth and not have defensive qualms about it. In Nelson's lifetime, he has had to build defenses against the revilement and abuse heaped upon the family until good works, the passage of time, and the organized resort to philanthropy won for old John's heirs and the Rockefeller name the respect, envy, and adulation which the fickle public, quick to scorn but eternally in search of heroes, transferred to them. Anyone seeking to discern the inner drives of a man like Nelson Rockefeller, or who tries to understand his enormous ambition to be President—and the colossal mistakes he has made in the attempt—cannot overlook the fact that he is, like all of us, to some degree a captive of the past. While experience and achievement add to a man's measure, he often remains nonetheless the vassal of old reflexes.

When Nelson was elected Governor of New York in 1958 and started his long and costly campaign to become President of the United States, it was generally acknowledged that his election to a high public office, twenty-one years after his grandfather's death, had capped the long process of absolving—indeed, of exalting—the family name. By the time John D., Sr., died in 1937, he had given away more than half a billion dollars, and his son—Nelson's father—who succeeded him as trustee of the Rockefeller fortune, had disbursed gifts to the total of $473,000,000 when he died in 1960 at the age of eighty-six. Not only the extent of the Rockefeller philanthropy, which was unparalleled in American history, but the quality and breadth of it, the far-reaching and humanitarian effects of it, evoked more than absolution. It commanded world-wide respect and helped establish both a high concept and an advanced professional standard for the use of private wealth in the public interest.

Nelson's emergence as an articulate and responsible public figure—a confident, attractive, appealing man who could not only charm the birds out of the trees but who exuded, to all appearances, qualities of leadership and boldness on a heroic but *sensible* scale—delighted and comforted the multitudes. It was interpreted by much of the press and the public as the kind of accomplishment money couldn't buy, but that had to be deserved and earned.

In the summer of 1930, Nelson married Mary Todhunter Clark, a Philadelphia socialite, granddaughter of the president of the Pennsylvania Railroad. Tod had been a vacation acquaintance in Maine, where the Clark and Rockefeller families maintained summer homes near each other. Tall and lean, a competent sportswoman with a free-swinging stride, she had become a friend of Nelson's by reason of proximity and suitability in the mannered, chaperoned environment of their time and status. The parents of the young couple would have preferred them to delay the marriage, according to reports published later, but consented to the wedding right after Nelson's graduation. Their wedding present from John and Abby Rockefeller was a one-year honeymoon trip around the world, which included many prearranged visits with heads of state, Standard Oil executives, and industrial leaders associated with Rockefeller enterprises. For Nelson it was a short course in foreign affairs and the beginning of his prolonged interest in both economic and social conditions—around the world— an interest doubtless intensified by the stock market crash and the deepening depression that was enveloping the United States.

Back home, the young marrieds settled into an apartment on East 67th Street and a newly remodeled house which had been prepared for them on the Pocantico Hills estate, a kind of baronial principality overlooking the Hudson River, twenty-six miles north of Manhattan. Nelson went to work at the Standard Oil offices at 26 Broadway— his first choice of innumerable opportunities open to him in the multitude of Rockefeller operations. The routine desk job bored him in a few months. He stayed with it, part-time, however, and with a friend began to explore Manhattan for more interesting possibilities. He established a business to lease office space in Rockefeller Center, a complex of buildings then going up in midtown Manhattan. The $125,000,000 building project, started by Nelson's father, needed a lot of tenants in those depression years when business in general was dangerously moribund, and competition among commercial landlords was ruthless. Nelson, thriving in an atmosphere of contest, enjoyed his job —especially when it allowed him to don a hard hat and preside over ceremonies celebrating construction progress.

Unfair leasing practices were charged against Rockefeller Center by August Heckscher, a millionaire builder and philanthropist. Nelson was accused of using leverage, in the form of price cutting and paying off unexpired leases, so that tenants could vacate their premises and move into his new buildings. A $10,000,000 damage suit filed by Heckscher was dropped, or just possibly settled out of court, before it went to trial. Nelson went on with his work and became president of Rockefeller Center in 1938. He was then thirty.

Concurrently, while in his mid-twenties, he was making long trips to Latin American countries, buying art, and making investments. He invested substantially in Creole Petroleum Company in Venezuela, ultimately developed other enterprises in that country, and established a great ranch near Valencia, to which he retreats for both relaxation and work, and to which he took Mrs. Margaretta Murphy Rockefeller for a honeymoon following their marriage in the spring of 1963.

Other published works and the public relations reports of oil companies have printed and advertised Nelson's activities in Latin America, and even though allowances must be made for the fervent and flattering accounts that paid hands prepare for the institutions which employ them, it seems quite clear that the young Mr. Rockefeller persuaded and goaded older executives in the petroleum industry to institute social and economic reforms in their industrial practices abroad. Executives were ordered to

21

learn the language of the country, company schools were built, health and sanitary conditions were improved, and the corporations that were developing and exploiting foreign natural resources were induced to return something of value to the lands that were adding to the riches of the oil industry. Corrupt and dictatorial governments, of course, had to be dealt with and the history of the twentieth century in many of the Latin American nations tells a sorry story of United States government and industrial power at work in the tradition-bound and impoverished nations of the Spanish (and Portuguese) speaking continent. Revolution, anarchy, and expropriation of foreign business were always just around the corner in most Latin American lands, but there seems to be little doubt that reforms instituted by certain U.S. corporations—reforms which Nelson Rockefeller helped bring about—had some effect in reducing Latin bitterness against the Yanquis.

With Hitler's Nazis decimating Europe, President Franklin D. Roosevelt called Nelson to Washington to draft a program to cope with Axis policies in South America. From 1940 to 1946 he headed an agency called the Office of the Coordinator of Inter-American Affairs, presiding at times over a staff of perhaps 1,500 employees and spending a total of $140,000,000.

The war threatened, through lost exports and Axis economic warfare, to destroy what remained of stability in Latin American nations. Rockefeller's agency, aided by his own knowledge of Latin American trade conditions, opened up channels for absorbing imports; it cost the United States premium prices, but it deprived the Axis powers of raw materials. American corporations were forced to sever connections with German agents, and anti-American espionage and propaganda were curtailed. Rockefeller got into trouble and was roundly rebuked by

22

President Roosevelt after a squabble with Under Secretary of State Sumner Welles, but he and his agency survived the internecine warfare of Washington and won the power to establish a propaganda and news service which directly supplied pro-Allied copy to 1,200 newspapers in Latin America. One method of getting the U.S. news copy printed was through the control Rockefeller held over newsprint exported from the U.S. Our friends got newsprint; neutral or unfriendly newspapers did not. U.S. movie producers were induced to withhold their feature films from motion picture houses that showed Axis news clips, and U.S. sound trucks carried American newsreels and movies to the Latin American countryside. Rockefeller circulated a pro-U.S. magazine, which grew by 1944 to a circulation of 548,000 and which is said to have opened the doors to the subsequent publication of Latin American editions of *Time* magazine and *Reader's Digest*. With the exception of Argentina, which was under the thumb of the notorious Juan Perón even before he was elected president in 1946, South America weathered the war on the Allied side.

Rockefeller was named Assistant Secretary of State for American Republics Affairs by President Roosevelt. It was in this elevated role that Rockefeller, in a battle against such an immovable force as John Foster Dulles and the brilliant secretary of the United Nations Conference, Alger Hiss, won acceptance for Argentina in the membership of the United Nations. Rockefeller's position was, simply, that Latin American unity was a precious asset of the future, plus the fact that the U.S. had given its word to support Argentina in return for stipulated concessions. For this victory in placing Perón's government in the U.N. among the more pro-U.S. nations of the hemisphere, Nelson Rockefeller endured nasty press attacks for being anti-Russian and "pro-Fascist."

He left the State Department in 1945 after it became

evident, in the Truman administration, that the United States had little intention of seeking accelerated social and economic development in Latin America. Almost alone, Rockefeller succeeded in getting the South American republics to accept the veto clause in the United Nations Charter. The whole idea was distasteful to them. Rockefeller's prestige, his fluency in Spanish, and his low-pressure persuasive tactics brought in seven votes in support of the veto, which the United States insisted upon, and two votes against it— from Colombia and Cuba. The other republics abstained.

When President Harry Truman sent Spruille Braden to Argentina as Ambassador, Rockefeller was finished in Washington. Perón, meeting his pledge in return for his U.N. seat, was holding national elections. Braden spoke against Peron, the latter cried "Yanqui interventionist" and cited past U.S. intrusions in Latin American affairs. Braden blundered and the delicate lines on which amity might have been developed were strained. Perón's fascination for fascism did not, in Latin American views, excuse the United States for throwing its weight around in an election held at U.S. insistence.

Rockefeller was scheduled to make a speech before the Pan American Society in Boston and wanted to talk about the developments in Argentina, on which he was certainly informed. He has said that he disagreed not with Braden's objectives but with his methods, though this seems an exercise in politeness. He must have been seething, knowing that Braden's conduct would infuriate nationalists and all levels of leadership among Latin America's 200,000,000 people. Whatever his true feelings were, he caught up with Secretary of State James Byrnes, on the latter's return from the Potsdam Conference in 1945, and advised him of the forthcoming Boston speech.

"The President is going to accept your resignation," Byrnes said.

Rockefeller retorted that he would make the speech as a private citizen, a role in which he would be free to speak more bluntly and truthfully than he might if bound by the restraint imposed on an Under Secretary of State.

Byrnes decided on the spot that Rockefeller restraint was preferable to the candor of a "resigned" private citizen. It must have been a tension-filled moment. Rockefeller's resignation as a State Department official was held up until after the speech.

"Mr. Rockefeller has been under unceasing and ill-informed criticism because of his part in forcing through an invitation of participation for Argentina," the *New York Times* declared in an editorial reporting on the Boston speech. It commended Rockefeller for accepting "the entire criticism of the San Francisco action. . . . He is respected everywhere in South America. It is hoped he will carry on unofficially as ambassador of good will."

Nelson Rockefeller was thirty-seven years old in 1945 when he was forced out of his appointed post in the federal government, and it did no credit to either President Truman or to Secretary of State Byrnes to let him go. On balance and with the clear help of hindsight, he was right and the quality and volume of his work were extraordinary. With real authority and power in the hands of others, he had demonstrated competence and a capacity for getting things accomplished, and he showed he had the essential toughness to rebound after rebukes and frustration to do the things he was charged with doing.

When a man is in public life he is visible, his performance is measurable—even though not everybody measures it with the same scale or arrives at the same result. But private life, even a private business, is visible only part of the time. And to a Rockefeller it is visible pretty much when he permits it to be. Thus in private ventures under-

25

taken by Rockefellers, we are dependent largely on the officially approved reports for information about them.

Until Nelson went back to Washington in President Truman's second term to become chairman of the International Advisory Board late in 1950, he was working mainly on two vast projects of his own. One was the American International Association for Economic Development and the other was International Basic Economy Corporation (AIA and IBEC) which were designed as private corporations to initiate development work in South America that the U.S. government itself might well have done.

AIA created self-help and managerial training projects in Brazil and Venezuela in association with local and regional governmental bodies. The Rockefeller brothers—John, Laurance, Nelson, Winthrop, and David—and their sister, Abby Rockefeller Mauze, provided the funds. Local authorities provided, when they could, matching funds, materials, personnel, and services. Trained home economists, agricultural specialists, health workers, and social workers taught and trained people in developing individual and community skills.

AIA was a remarkable, perhaps unrealistic, example of good intentions, effort, and expenditure of resources. Its successes, fewer than its failures, were notable, if isolated. One of the principal rewards was educational—for the administrators. Nelson Rockefeller devoted enormous energy to these projects; and Mrs. Mauze and the brothers and participating governments put $15,000,000 into them. An appraisal of this imaginative and charitable operation is not possible here; yet in its nobility of purpose and the willingness to risk resources in undertaking it, it was a monumental act of goodness.

IBEC was something else again. Set up in 1947, it was

26

designed to attract investors to finance remunerative enterprises in South America, meanwhile adding to the employment rolls and the economy of the host country. It was an effort to organize private enterprise in profit-making ventures by attracting native capital, stimulating production of goods, and developing management communities in the areas of its operations. IBEC started out with $4,750,000 of Rockefeller money and with three or four times that amount committed by corporations, most of them responsive to Rockefeller influence.

The bright, handsomely designed supermarkets seen today in Venezuela emerged from the IBEC money and talent resources. There are probably a dozen of them, some more architecturally imaginative and elegant than those in the United States, standing like monumental showcases in Caracas. They have, of course, revolutionized food distribution and upgraded processing and food handling standards. Supermarkets are spreading around the world now, as IBEC operations have expanded to other continents. The corporation made no money for about five years, but has been making a profit since 1958 in housing projects, agricultural processing plants, textile mills, food freezing operations, and so on. There can be no doubt that it has functioned as a privately financed foreign aid program in a demonstration that tied the profit motive to economic development in many countries. IBEC says its program inspired the so-called Point Four foreign aid concept enunciated by President Truman, and this may very well be true. Nelson Rockefeller was so enthusiastic about the Truman Point Four program that he initiated with the President a thinly veiled attempt to help promote and develop it, but Truman snubbed him, at least for the moment.

In the days when Nelson was getting AIA and IBEC

27

established, he made repeated field trips to out-of-the-way places in Latin America. He was lionized at social functions and warmly received almost everywhere. Mrs. Rockefeller, who had by this time borne five children—Ann, Steven, Rodman, and the twins Michael and Mary—was not involved in Nelson's work. Full staffs of people buzzed about the quiet offices at 30 Rockefeller Plaza, the U.S. headquarters of the AIA-IBEC, where reports were funneled out to, and received from, an array of Latin American projects. It was a closely knit organization in which the stay-at-home administrative staff, at least, got to know each other well. From Latin American outposts they sometimes heard filtered gossip that Nelson was living it up south of the border. It was said that in New York he appeared to be almost lonesome at times. He would show up at small gatherings alone and was introduced as "Mr. Nelson" to guests who did not recognize him, or at least pretended not to. Possibly this was a discreet form of incognito to spare him boring and repetitious conversations with people who might have been ill at ease in, or might have overreacted to, the company of Nelson Rockefeller.

A young woman who worked on the staff was his friend. A cool and stunning girl, she was the beneficiary of what others, perhaps jealously, construed to be special privileges and consideration. As a dynamic and exposed public figure, Nelson would doubtless have welcomed a trusted confidante—one among the staff capable of and willing to shield his confidences from more gossipy subordinates. In any case, the young lady eventually married; her husband was given a well-paid assignment in Latin America and she continued, for a time, to work on the New York staff.

Nelson was then, as now, a most attractive man. He

weighed perhaps 175 or 180 pounds (and looks just slightly heavier now), with dark eyes, broad shoulders, and a well-muscled frame. An osteopath came to his hideaway office-lounge on the fifty-seventh floor at 30 Rockefeller once or twice a week to administer treatments. He also had his Spanish lessons there, for, while he was competent in the language, he sought always to improve.

Most people around him liked and admired him, and expressed it in circumspect and sometimes flippant ways. Quips and office jokes acknowledged both his great wealth and the attractiveness he had for women. Late one morning, a tall, svelte staff worker paused at a window overlooking the Plaza and watched a cortege of armored trucks pulling up, single file, to a bank entrance, apparently to make some large transfer or delivery to the vaults. The girl called several other women over to the window, and, pointing to the scene below, wisecracked:

"Here they come with Nelson's lunch money."

No indiscretions or breaches of conduct were ever specifically attributed to Nelson at that time, although it was now and then observed by subordinates and associates that he did not appear to be happy at home. Subjective conclusions unsupported by corroboration are nothing more than speculative gossip, an example of which might be the pointed observation, emanating from a source that suffers from mandatory anonymity, that Tod Rockefeller was obliged to "file and forget" the rumors that reached her through channels of court whisperings.

When Dwight D. Eisenhower was elected president in 1952, Nelson Rockefeller, then forty-four years old and a savvy veteran of the federal bureaucracy, went into the government with him, as Chairman of the President's

Advisory Committee on Government Organization. Others in the three-man agency were the president's brother, Dr. Milton Eisenhower, and Dr. Arthur S. Flemming.

Among the many proposals for government reorganization made by the team was the blueprint for the Department of Health, Education and Welfare. Mrs. Oveta Culp Hobby was named Secretary and Nelson became an Under Secretary. In HEW, Rockefeller was frequently drubbed by, and fought back against, the hard-nosed "money savers" of the Eisenhower administration: Treasury Secretary George Humphrey, Under Secretary of State Herbert Hoover, Jr., and Budget Director Rowland Hughes, among others. Most of these clashes had to do with budget requests made by HEW which the business-oriented administration leaders tried to slash. Then the American Medical Association marshaled its vested power against Rockefeller and the HEW over the department's insurance scheme designed to ease the catastrophe of costly medical bills to the poor. The AMA, as usual, suggested that such an idea was socialistic and Rockefeller's humanitarian position won for him a clobbering from the uncompromising AMA.

All attempts on the part of Rockefeller and the HEW to put the federal government behind medical care and education fell on deaf ears, for the most part, during both terms of the Eisenhower administration. In education, the need was great, but not until Soviet Russia put its Sputnik into space in 1957 did the government consider the educational and medical programs that had been desperately needed for many years. Rockefeller quit HEW to become a Special Assistant to Eisenhower. His field was foreign affairs.

It remains vague to this day exactly what Rockefeller's responsibilities were in 1955 when he attended meetings of the National Security Council, the Cabinet, and other high level policy-making bodies. Much of his work was secret; it involved strategy and planning in the cold war. It also evoked obstructionist tactics from Herbert Hoover, Jr., and Secretary of State John Foster Dulles, neither of whom approved of Nelson's being given a hand in foreign policy. Nevertheless, he helped President Eisenhower formulate the "Open Skies" nuclear arms proposal which Ike unveiled, with Rockefeller in attendance, at the Geneva Summit Conference in mid-1955.

His last official job before he resigned at the end of that year was to submit a report, based on the dialogue and reports of two secret seminars he had organized to explore cold war and foreign aid strategy. The classified report has never been made public, although it became known that it proposed a six-year co-ordinated program calling for expenditures of $18 billion. This was less than the cost of programs then going forward, but Secretary Humphrey thought the tab was too high.

Rockefeller departed to try to become President of the United States, a goal that meant becoming Governor of New York first.

Machiavelli in the Making

2

Real political power in the United States lies with the elected, not the elect. The highest level of that power is in the office of the President of the United States, of which President Harry Truman has said, "The buck stops here." (A small desk sign on which these four words were printed confronted all visitors to Mr. Truman's office.) But in American slang, buck has two common meanings. It is the evaded decision passed upward to the level where decision is inescapable—and it is money. Nelson Rockefeller had more of it than any man before him who ever advanced toward the presidency, not excluding that other expert in the use of money in the pursuit of the same goal, John Fitzgerald Kennedy.

The presidency, of course, cannot be achieved through money alone. If it could, William Randolph Hearst, who, in addition to great wealth, had absolute command over a privately owned newspaper and communications empire, would probably have won the office.

Similarities between Nelson Rockefeller and John F. Kennedy were less real than apparent; they were reflected on the surface of American political life, not in its depth. The Kennedys were steeped in politics—in the precincts, in the wards of Boston, in the State of Massachusetts, in

32

Congress and the Senate—and two Kennedy brothers, Robert and Ted, still labor restlessly in the political vineyards, awaiting a vintage year. By contrast, Nelson Rockefeller came along in the off season and bought the crop from a man named L. Judson Morhouse. It was a bitter wine that ripened, although Nelson survived the aftertaste while Morhouse was decanted from public life.

Judson Morhouse was State Chairman of the Republican Party and the political power figure of the minority party in New York when Rockefeller blossomed into a gubernatorial candidate in 1955 and 1956. The two met appropriately enough at a Republican fund-raising dinner in the wintertime of the party's hopes late in 1955. It was a fortuitous meeting for both of them, for what each possessed the other needed.

The cheerful and politically cagey Morhouse, a tall, crew-cut lawyer from the Ticonderoga country on Lake Champlain in upper New York, had been installed as State Chairman by former Governor Thomas E. Dewey in 1954, and bore the identification of "Dewey's boy" (he was not yet forty when chosen) with aplomb. Dewey's defeat by President Truman had diminished his luster but not his party control in New York State. Morhouse's first important job was to collect the pieces and put things together again after Averell Harriman, a Democratic millionaire who had stood in Nelson's way in Washington a couple of times, was elected Governor in 1954. True, Harriman's election over Irving Ives had been a cliffhanger—the margin was 11,000 votes—but it put the Republicans out of rule after twelve golden years. Morhouse wanted the GOP to reoccupy the great gray fortress capital at Albany, and Nelson Rockefeller, who had got his boot training under three presidents in Washington, seemed a perfect contender for the 1958 fray. Morhouse staked his job and his future on Rockefeller by inducing the jaded GOP in New York to accept the intruder.

It is perhaps not out of context to reflect, ten years afterward, on that fusion of interests and ambitions that was clearly visible when Judson Morhouse and Nelson Rockefeller became partners in a common cause. Both were young men on the go, both were in their forties, presentable, and confident. Morhouse was one of the diminishing assembly of self-made lawyers. He had read law in an attorney's office in Ticonderoga until he passed the bar examination. He was a country boy from a small town in the north who, by diligence, good luck, and personality, had risen to an enviable political position.

A quartet of state Republican claimants was maneuvering for the gubernatorial nomination in 1958, including men like former national GOP chairman Leonard Hall and the Republican State Senate leader, Walter J. Mahoney. These Old Guard types could not be depended upon to be responsive, in specific terms, to the Morhouse hopes and aspirations. Besides, if any of the present crop of hopefuls was to get the nomination—and win—Morhouse would be only one of many deserving Republicans with a claim on the rewards. But if Rockefeller could be engineered into the winner's spot, doubtful as it looked through that early haze, a lot of in-group opposition would be euchred out of position on award night. If the team isn't paying much attention to the coach, well, send in a new man.

As for Rockefeller, he may have been an intruder in the electoral sweepstakes, without prior experience or association in the clubhouse set, but he was scarcely an outsider. He was very well known—a factor that Morhouse exploited brilliantly—and he had been, with his family, a

34

source of financial strength in contributions to the party. He, too, could be expected to welcome a situation in which developing internecine competition might be resolved by a peacemaker with a better chance of winning than any of the contenders—if the troublesome nomination could be achieved.

Up to then, what Rockefeller had done with his vast wealth was, indirectly in some cases but nevertheless demonstrably, in the public interest.

Rockefeller was a clean, vigorous, novice politician who might well have felt that he did not need the years of elemental rehearsal in vote-getting, any more than a cat needs practice climbing a tree. And on top of everything else, he had instant resources to throw into the fray, to do the research, to help him become an expert on the state, and to provide the whole body of dialogue and literature that, combined with his own attractiveness, and energy, and money, could scarcely be matched by all the other candidates put together.

The Democratic nominee was Averell Harriman, a lesser millionaire, but his fires seemed somewhat banked and, despite formidable Democratic strength in the electorate, he could surely be put on the defensive because of the Tammany Hall "bossism" issue in New York. Nelson need not have seen himself as a Galahad or even as a Kennedy, but he would have had short vision, indeed, had he not measured these elements and concluded that all he had to lose was what he had plenty of. Just work with Morhouse, get the communications program going, and he could climb the hill at Albany, from which, when the climate is right, every New York governor glimpses the shimmering outlines of the distant White House.

Rockefeller and Morhouse were worlds apart, but each

was the key to the other's needs. Together, they were successful in what they set out to do. In time, Mr. Morhouse was caught, shamed, and convicted,* but by then Nelson Rockefeller didn't need him any more.

In 1956 Morhouse, proceeding with what was becoming an irreversible commitment, maneuvered Rockefeller onto the fifteen-man State Commission for a Constitutional Convention to study reapportionment and proposed changes in the state constitution. Governor Harriman was empowered to name the chairman and while it was a little astonishing that he chose Rockefeller, it was rationalized on the grounds that Nelson had less reason than any of the ten Democrats or four other Republicans on the Commission to try to rig a reapportionment scheme to the competitive hopes of either political party.

For Rockefeller, it was a piece of good fortune handed to him on a platter by the man he was to defeat two years hence. With his own staff conducting studies, making surveys, and interviewing experts, Rockefeller was the beneficiary of a vast reservoir of data. He called on Dr. William J. Ronan, dean of the School of Public Administration of New York University, to help him. The educator was joined by a Binghamton lawyer and political specialist, George Hinman. Back at the office in Rockefeller Center he had the counsel, brains, and dedication of another good man, Francis Jamieson, a highly competent journalist who handled the Rockefeller public relations operations.

Nelson, as Commission Chairman, amassing and digesting the literature and mechanics of reapportionment, traveled all over the state, conferring with politicians,

* As this book goes to press, Morhouse's lawyer has said the conviction will be appealed.

educators, and workers of both parties. It was a kind of preliminary gubernatorial campaign which, while subordinate to his assigned purpose, gave him a trotting start up that hill in Albany. He would, of course, have to keep going—but Judson Morhouse was right behind him all the time.

After the Commission voted to kill the proposed constitutional convention on reapportionment, the structure of which was ultimately defined as a one-man, one-vote principle by the U.S. Supreme Court, Morhouse began leaking the results of some political sampling polls. They showed, not at all surprisingly, that the name of Nelson Rockefeller was better known in the state than the names of other contenders for the nomination: Hall, Mahoney, et al. The polls doubtless would have shown that the Rockefeller name was well known in Russia, too, but it was the *use* to which Morhouse put the poll-taking findings that helped his cause. By selling Nelson's ascendant popularity to political leaders, Morhouse deterred them from investing time, energy, and resources in other contenders. Some of them were furious, and charged Morhouse with favoritism in what was supposed to be a neutral role. Morhouse explained blandly that he was only passing on factual reports.

The opposition withered, the Old Guard raged—and Nelson formally announced his candidacy for the nomination. He said he had a "deep conviction that a new approach to government must be taken in New York State. . . . What we need is a transfusion of political courage to grasp the opportunities and ideas of men who have convictions and creative talent, and faith in the future."

On August 7, he was nominated and enthusiastically acclaimed at the state GOP convention in Buffalo. As his running mate for Lieutenant Governor, he took on Assemblyman Malcolm Wilson, a strong man in the Legislature, an orator whose tone is faintly reminiscent of Boston's James Curley. Wilson had a law firm in Yonkers and was known throughout the state. He was conservative enough to be a liaison man in the Legislature for Cardinal Spellman. With Wilson giving balm to the Old Guard, and Rockefeller, unsullied by previous identity with state Republican factions, armed to capture defecting Democrats and the independent vote, a whirlwind campaign for Governor began.

The "battle of the millionaires" was something to remember. Rockefeller crisscrossed the state in his own airplane, carrying with him bound and indexed volumes containing digests of exhaustive studies made by staff people and by both volunteer and hired experts.* He charged Harriman with inaction and indecisiveness, high budgets, rising taxes, subservience to "bosses," and running up an enormous deficit that would bring on a "crisis." He said there was too much organized crime and juvenile delinquency, not enough housing, inadequate health and welfare services, congested traffic conditions, and so on.

Harriman tried to campaign against the Eisenhower administration and broadly hinted that Rockefeller had an agreement to run for Vice President with Richard Nixon in 1960. Rockefeller said the idea of *his* taking second place on a Nixon ticket was "absolute fantasy," and, anyway, he didn't have any interest in running for President, let alone Vice President.

Both Nixon and President Eisenhower were courteously but firmly invited out of the campaign in New York in about the same manner and for perhaps the same reasons that Rockefeller himself was encouraged to stay out of the

* One of the many volunteer workers for Rockefeller at this time was Mrs. Margaretta Murphy, wife of a medical scientist and a friend and admirer of Rockefeller.

John Lindsay campaign for Mayor in New York in 1965. The reasoning is that some "help" doesn't really help at all.*

Morhouse managed the team, with public relations man Francis Jamieson presiding over the circuit as a kind of working chairman of the board; legislative strongman Wilson worked in the field where the party regulars were playing it close, and television—lots and lots of television —covered it all.

Nelson popped up in every one of the state's sixty-two counties, making hundreds of informal talks and 135 formal ones in more than 100 towns and cities. He chewed candy and ate rubber chicken, wore funny hats, hugged people, and said, "Hi, I'm Nelson Rockefeller," thousands of times. He was folksy, friendly, serious, ebullient, direct, informed, and indefatigable. He got a wonderful, favorable press and he won over Harriman by 530,000 votes.

Rockefeller's inaugural address in Albany sounded like a presidential campaign speech. He was on top of the hill. Down yonder, maybe two or maybe six years away, was the White House.

The law of New York State requires a balanced budget. Rockefeller had charged Harriman with inducing the worst financial crisis in thirty years by spending funds intended for aid to education and welfare, and by borrowing. The history of municipal and state government is pock-marked

---

* Rockefeller apparently made a substantial contribution, both in terms of staff and cash, to Lindsay's successful campaign for Mayor of New York in 1965. He was not permitted to enter the temple, however. Early reports were that Nelson had pledged $500,000 to Lindsay's effort, but second-echelon Lindsay people scoffed at this and said the contribution could not have exceeded $100,000. Robert Price, a very able man who managed Rockefeller's primary campaign in Oregon before he managed Lindsay's mayoralty campaign, did not care to discuss either Rockefeller or money. And talking about money with Rockefeller people seems, at best, like a breach of etiquette.

with cutting criticism of fiscal policies allowing the dissipation of earmarked funds for current expenses. A classic case is the money raised by bond issues to build the Second Avenue Subway in New York City. The money, $500 million, was raised in the 1950s but it is all gone now and there is no subway. The charge against Harriman, who had been in office only one term after twelve years of GOP control, was that he had led the state into a financial mess which Rockefeller intended to clean up.

Rockefeller cut $300 million from Harriman's proposed budget of $2.3 billion. The cut seemed a great deal larger than the amount of the deficit Rockefeller had predicted. He had said that the program he had in mind to stimulate economic expansion would bring in added revenues, yet a deficit was *still* certain. He asked for new taxes in the amount of $277 million, including an increase of $150 million in state income taxes that would compel 300,000 low-income families not then paying taxes to start doing so. He got the bill through the Legislature, after some budget trimming and a provision to ease the burden for people with the lowest incomes.

Then, in his first term of office, a bomb shelter mania struck Nelson Rockefeller. He seemed to want every house and building in the state to erect some kind of concrete or block container and stock it with food and water so that people would have something to crawl into in the event of a nuclear attack. One of many fact-finding and advisory groups he had appointed—there were about fifty all told—sold him on the idea with reasoning that must have been more frightening than objective. In any case, he went before the Legislature to request enormous sums of money and authority to put as much as possible of the state underground, or under cover, as a protection against the final doom.

40

A good deal of abuse characterized the dialogue on this issue. The main body of opinion scoffed at the use of tax funds to wall off and reinforce sections of basement, install filters and "radiation-resistant" roofs to slow up the effects of fallout. While some "experts," largely civil defense appointees and military spokesmen, declared that we ought to make plans to save enough lives to begin reprocreation in nuclear-destroyed areas, those less responsive to the shelter idea questioned the effectiveness of such enclosures in any region subject to vaporization and damned the war psychosis that emphasized futile protective programs.

A good deal of debate developed over the morality of bomb shelter conduct on Bomb Day. The question of whether a citizen—prudent enough to build a well-stocked private shelter (complete with generator, hi-fi, reading material and fun-and-games equipment to while away the weeks while radiation was diminishing)—had the right to shoot and kill some apartment dweller or out-of-town visitor who might try to crowd in was seriously discussed by some people, but in general it drew revulsion or guffaws.

Nelson Rockefeller was in deadly earnest about his program, however, and did not desist in attempts to implement it until the Legislature declined to go along.

Even without the money, some aspects of the shelter mania went forward. At a given signal, children in schools were compelled to crawl under their desks and remain there until the simulated danger period had passed. This was known in Civil Defense circles as the "duck-and-cover" period, which has now given way to drills in which the children march off to some designated corner. Most adult citizens, many of whom protested the duck-and-cover period at the time, have probably forgotten this governmentally inspired nonsense, but apparently the children's memories of curling up on the floor with their hands over their eyes have lingered. On television interviews and news shows related to the "teach-ins" and marches protesting U.S. policy in Viet Nam, some of the younger New York peaceniks, as they were pejoratively called, remembered crystallizing their antiwar views in the hush and self-imposed blackout of their duck-and-cover days.

Rockefeller's own determination to promote his bomb shelter doctrine was not curtailed, but it did undergo a change of direction when the Legislature turned down his bill. Subsequently, he had a top level New York engineering firm, which had done some feasibility and design studies for Rockefeller interests at Dorado Beach in Puerto Rico and in the Virgin Islands, design a state office building four miles from the Capitol at Albany on the site of the State University. The engineering firm, Praeger-Kavanagh-Waterbury, had an impeccable background related to shelter design: under the direction of one of the firm's senior partners, Charles Morrissey, a blast-resistant complex was built three storeys underground to house government officials and their departments. Mr. Morrissey had excellent credentials for the project; he had designed "hard" underground missile launching sites at secret locations to withstand all but direct hits from nuclear projectiles.

The three-storey underground structure was the foundation, which could be sealed off, for a conventional state office building aboveground. The completed underground chambers, stocked with supplies, were prepared to house several hundred essential workers and defense specialists in crowded safety for several weeks, after which they could presumably emerge and check on how the school kids under the desks made out.

It is now understood that the building will be taken

42

over by the State University. Cost of construction was about $8 million.

When the economic recessions of the Eisenhower administration gave way to business revival and expansion, Rockefeller proclaimed that his administration had reversed the "flight of industry" from New York State and that sound "pay-as-you-go" fiscal policy, painfully achieved through tax increases, had put the state on a solid, safe foundation. The financial crisis was over, and he promised no further tax increases. State aid was increased to local school districts and to the people, on whom the taxes had been levied in the first place. The unemployment rate, which had increased in the preceding national recessions, dropped as the boom times of 1962 approached.

Long overdue legislation on civil rights, minimum wages, housing, and enforcement of laws against slumlords were passed between 1958 and 1962. These were a response to mounting human requirements in congested urban areas. Rockefeller later set up construction schemes which he said were paid for by private investments without using any state funds or credit. In point of fact, this is not true. His formula for using private money, with interest charges to the state, kept the bills from showing on the balance sheet, which produced the legally required balanced budget and false evidence of pay-as-you-go. Before long Rockefeller was doing what he'd charged Harriman with doing. The budget only *appeared* to be balanced.

Throughout much of Rockefeller's first term in Albany, there were voices raised in protest. Legislators carped that his privately organized task forces were usurping the powers of public deliberative and fact-finding bodies. In Rockefeller's defense, however, it must be reported that

43

legislative committees at times tend to confuse personal and party politics with objectivity and public needs. For a Governor in a hurry, who has himself become well informed on legislative necessities, this can be a disillusioning and frustrating experience.

One of the more consistent voices of protest against Rockefeller's fiscal manipulations was Arthur Levitt, the State Comptroller. Then and now the chief official responsible for audit and control of state finances charged the Governor with misrepresenting fiscal facts to the public. He disputed Nelson's contention that no new tax money would have to be raised by the state and declared that the pay-as-you-go doctrine was, in effect, spurious. In the press from time to time there appeared reports suggesting that a difference in fact existed between the fiscal policy as defined by Nelson Rockefeller and the fiscal policy that actually prevailed.

Some legislators winced at Nelson's no-tax pledge, but then they, like Arthur Levitt, were Democrats and their trustworthiness as critics was diluted by the possibility of partisanship. One of the top men in the administration, Keith McHugh, admitted in the privacy of his own office that he "wished Nelson hadn't said that"—meaning the no-tax commitment. Mr. McHugh is the former President of the New York Telephone Company and, of course, a Republican. He went into the state government with Nelson as Commissioner of the Department of Commerce and was one of the men around Nelson who very early saw in Senator Goldwater a dangerous threat to Rockefeller's aspirations.

Objections to the Governor's private task force activities diminished as the Rockefeller staff turned to presidential, as differentiated from gubernatorial, matters.

44

Immediately after the first legislative session was well under way, Dr. William Ronan, a former New York University professor who had become Nelson's Secretary and Administrative Officer, and Lieutenant Governor Malcolm Wilson took over management of the Albany shop. Nelson and the rest of his staff devoted themselves to the job of getting the Republican nomination for the presidency.

Throughout 1959, GOP convention delegates were recruited; Rockefeller made pointed speeches on national and foreign affairs before well-publicized forums. Public favor seemed to be developing for Nelson, but it was not transferable to the cold hearts of delegates. The Republican Old Guard, to whom Nelson was a middle-of-the-road moderate, and the right wing, to whom he was anathema, held the power. Richard Nixon had the equivocal but publicly stated support of President Eisenhower. "That's my boy!" Ike proclaimed after Nixon appeared with his wife and dog on a famed, tear-jerking television broadcast to explain the source of some questionable campaign funds.

On the evidence as subsequently analyzed—and certainly in the opinion of the nation's independent voters— Rockefeller was the superior candidate for the GOP nomination. Everybody thought so but the Republican delegates. William Ronan persuaded Nelson that the fight was hopeless. Nelson dropped out of the race and Nixon got the nomination.

Rockefeller came to feel, in time, that Ronan's counsel had been grievously wrong. Nevertheless, Ronan's opinion was nearly always sought by Rockefeller and the Secretary remained a power behind the throne in the Executive Chamber, even to the point that Ronan virtually served as Governor in Nelson's many absences from Albany. Ronan's services were rewarded in 1965 when Rockefeller appointed him to a $45,000 job as chairman of the Metropolitan Transportation Authority. It wasn't a conventional appointment, however. State legislation, which Rockefeller put through and signed, designated Ronan for the job and stipulated the salary, eliminating any chance of things going wrong for Bill Ronan on his long-term lucrative job. Legislators grumbled that the former Secretary's counsel scarcely merited such handsome treatment but they were relieved at what they called "the decline and fall of the Ronan empire."

On a repeated promise that there would be no more tax increases in the state for another four years—and on the pledge that state finances were secure—Rockefeller was re-elected Governor in 1962 over the more or less unknown Robert S. Morgenthau, U.S. District Attorney in southern New York and son of the late Henry Morgenthau, Jr., who had served in Franklin D. Roosevelt's Cabinet as Secretary of the Treasury.

Rockefeller's second inaugural address in 1962 was, in part, another presidential campaign speech, but its emphasis this time was not so much on international affairs as on domestic matters. For one thing, Senator Barry Goldwater had to be reckoned with. Thus Nelson spoke of extravagance in government and acknowledged that it was his "affirmative duty ruthlessly to prune out wasteful and nonessential expenditures of the taxpayers' money." He issued a clear call for "freedom" and paid homage to "the old-fashioned virtues." He pledged solemnly and confidently that there would be no new taxes, and called for "cooperation . . . to preserve the state's fiscal integrity."

Judson Morhouse was not among the guests at the second inaugural ceremony. Prominent among the elected

46

elite were Malcolm Wilson and the re-elected State Attorney General, Louis Lefkowitz. Also on hand was Carl Spad, who as a youth had grown up in a village near the Rockefeller holdings in Pocantico Hills. He was Nelson's Appointments (i.e., patronage) Secretary and was to succeed, on Rockefeller's command, to the post of State Chairman of the Republican Party, the job Judson Morhouse had had when he and Rockefeller discovered each other.

Rockefeller had given Morhouse a plum in the form of a $17,000-a-year job with the State Thruway Authority, which allowed him to go about his law business both in Ticonderoga and in New York City, where the State Liquor Authority, an agency in which he was interested, had its headquarters at 270 Broadway. The chairman of the SLA was Martin C. Epstein of Brooklyn, an appointee of Rockefeller's and a kind of subservant to Judson Morhouse.

"A man is known by the company he keeps" is an old-fashioned maxim that comes to people's minds when someone's associates are accused of having, in addition to feet of clay, sticky fingers. There is both treachery and nonsense in dependence upon such simplistic concepts. Judgment of a man by the shortcomings of his fellows is, except in special circumstances, unfair.

Nevertheless, a few days after Rockefeller was re-elected, New York District Attorney, Frank S. Hogan—*not* the State Attorney General's office—announced that a long investigation had turned up evidence of corruption in the State Liquor Authority and that its $24,000-a-year chairman, Martin Epstein, had failed to answer a subpoena. Judge Saul S. Streit signed an order to have Epstein examined by a doctor to determine whether he was sufficiently recovered from a leg amputation to face questioning.

47

Long before the liquor scandals came into public view, it was virtually common knowledge that the liquor licensing system and the enforcement of regulations applicable to bars were rife with corruption. The number of liquor stores had been frozen for fifteen years; no new stores could be opened until the would-be operator could arrange to obtain an already existing license. It was necessary to have the transfer approved by the State Liquor Authority. Lawyers with a reputation for obtaining favorable decisions from the SLA were considered a special resource in the New York liquor business. And it was perfectly permissible for a lawyer on the state payroll to appear before the SLA in behalf of a client, for a fee.

District Attorney Hogan was quoted in the *New York Times* as saying that obtaining a license for a package store, which sells liquor by the bottle, cost the operator $10,000 in graft "or gratuities." Similarly, a bar owner needed legal representation in proceedings resulting from alleged violations of SLA regulations—selling to minors, failure to serve food (as then required by law), permitting his premises to be used for solicitation by prostitutes, diluting the whiskey, and so on. Since such allegations could result in license revocations or suspensions, bar owners were highly motivated to obtain the services, or win the influence of, people with the right connections. The lawyer or the politician who earned the reputation of being "the man to see" had a steady flow of incoming business. Judson Morhouse was one of these.

In the past, Louis Lefkowitz had been an expert in handling legal cases before the liquor authorities. Mr. Lefkowitz's expertise in such matters seemed to fail him following his election as Attorney General, for apparently he never noticed the network of corruption spreading through the field in which he had been so familiar. True, as Attorney General he did not institute prosecutions; that was not his function. Attorney General Lefkowitz had substantial investigatory powers, however. The Governor's office, too, had great watchdog power over the conduct of miscreants, especially since Mr. Rockefeller had appointed most of them in the first place.

A former law associate of Mr. Lefkowitz's, Hyman D. Siegel, was indicted on charges of conspiring to bribe officials of the State Liquor Authority. He was mentioned by the prosecutor in the Morhouse case as the lawyer who first sought a liquor license for the Playboy Club. Mr. Siegel was still representing clients before the SLA in March, 1966. A *New York Times* story of May 4, 1966, reported that Mr. Siegel had returned a $5,000 fee to his client, the Playboy Club.

Messrs. Rockefeller and Lefkowitz appeared to know absolutely nothing about the state's corrupt liquor operations until informed of the business by District Attorney Frank Hogan in Manhattan.* It was fortunate that the SLA headquarters were located in Manhattan, where Mr. Hogan had jurisdiction to investigate and prosecute; otherwise the culprits might never have been detected and news of corruption might not have reached the Governor or the Attorney General at all.

To this day Epstein has never been brought to trial although both he and his wife are under indictment. Mrs. Epstein was caught on charges of entering her husband's office, with permission to pick up his personal effects, and walking off with incriminating files. When last heard from,

---

* Mr. Lefkowitz's office has been subject to other embarrassments. On April 21, 1966, District Attorney Hogan announced the indictment of an Assistant State Attorney General on charges of trying to shake down the owners of the National Book Club in Glen Cove, L. I., for $15,000. A year earlier, another Assistant Attorney General and an investigator were suspended after they were arrested and charged with the attempted shakedown of a Brooklyn undertaker.

the Epsteins were living in Florida where he remains an aged immobilized invalid.

Morhouse resigned his $17,000-a-year sinecure, as well as other unpaid but influential state connections, late in 1962. He said he wanted to devote more time to his family and his law practice. Epstein automatically lost his job after he declined to waive immunity and go before the grand jury. Another twenty or so lesser job holders in the SLA, most of them in the six-to-eight-thousand-a-year bracket, were also fired in the wake of the grand jury exposure. One of them committed suicide.

The departure of Morhouse coincided with reports that the Playboy Club, a real estate and socio-sexual offshoot of the lucrative *Playboy* magazine publishing venture, had to pay a stiff bribe to get its New York State liquor license. The club had also been denied a cabaret license by the New York City License Commissioner, a regulatory body that concerns itself with the jokes entertainers tell in night clubs and with the scantiness of the clothing worn by waitresses and performers. The City Commissioner seemed to think that the real scandal of the Playboy Club was its hostesses and waitresses, called Playboy Bunnies, who wear impractical, but provocative, clothes. Their costumes consist of protruding white ears, a stiff white collar, propped up breasts naked to the areola, and a kind of padded diaper covering taboo areas front and rear while leaving the sides bare to the belt. Caught at the buttocks is a kind of bouncy cotton tail. The whole costume is a failure; they still look like girls. The License Commissioner figured that too much girl showed through the disguise—so, no license.*

---

* The Playboy Club finally got its city cabaret license in December of 1965, partly as a reward for being "cooperative" in the liquor investigations, and partly for promising not to let the Bunnies "mingle" with the customers.

At the operating, or investment, level of the Playboy Club, the situation was also too much. The bribe price of its liquor license was $150,000.

In April 1963, the attorney for Judson Morhouse disclosed that his client had received $18,000 from Playboy for services rendered. A comfortable three years and several elections after Epstein was ousted, Morhouse himself was indicted. In December, 1965, he pleaded not guilty to charges of bribery and conspiracy and was paroled to await trial.

When Morhouse resigned in 1962 he said that he had "never done anything wrong" and denied interceding for anyone to help obtain a liquor license. "Who can remember what you did in eight years!" he asked. "I never interceded improvidently." Governor Rockefeller, reported the newspapers, accepted the resignation of his old sponsor with "regrets." There was no other comment. Frank Gervasi, in his presidential campaign biography of the Governor, said Rockefeller "fired" Morhouse. This is unsubstantiated in the published record.

A Chicago public relations man, Ralph Berger, figured in the Playboy bribe case as a contact man between the Playboy operations and Morhouse, according to records of a 1964 trial which led to a one-year jail sentence for Berger. He was charged with conspiring to bribe Epstein. By "cooperating" with the District Attorney, Berger has remained free on bail.

In the Berger trial, the prosecutor declared that Morhouse had "demanded" $100,000 for himself in five annual $20,000 payments, and $50,000 for Epstein in return for a liquor license for the 59th Street Playboy Club. The prosecutor quoted Morhouse as saying to Berger:

"Don't worry if you can't work things out with Epstein. He's soon up for retirement and I can appoint the next

SLA chairman. If that doesn't work, we can always change the law." *

Epstein was "Morhouse's stooge," according to District Attorney Hogan's chief assistant, Alfred J. Scotti, who handled the Morhouse indictment. Thus Morhouse appeared to have a right to be confident that he could name a new SLA chairman. At the time the District Attorney said Morhouse was demanding $100,000, plus some additional fringe benefits in stock and Playboy Club concession franchises, he was still State Chairman of the Republican Party and exercised what, on the record, appears to be the real power in the State Liquor Authority. He did not resign until the end of 1962, three months after being elected to his fifth consecutive term as State Chairman. His resignation received little public notice since it occurred when all of the New York and nearby Long Island newspapers were shut down in a 114-day strike. The Playboy Club got its liquor license at that time, too.

It appears that the only part of the $100,000 he personally received ultimately was that $18,000 reported by his attorney, Sol Gelb. One payment was made by a check drawn on the HMH Publishing Company, publisher of *Playboy* magazine and run by Hugh M. Hefner. The date was August 22, 1961. Another check was issued on March 15, 1962, to "Lyman Associates, Inc.," which was a corporate euphemism for Morhouse.

In the spring of 1963, *Life* magazine published an article summarizing the details of the Playboy case. The article disclosed and documented evidence that other prom-

* The quotation was read by Assistant District Attorney Jeremiah B. McKenna and republished in a news account of the Morhouse indictment in the *New York Herald Tribune,* December 8, 1965. Mr. McKenna is now in private law practice.

52

inent Republicans had received fees for representing clients before SLA hearings while serving in high positions. Republican Majority Leader Walter J. Mahoney, who had been a leading aspirant for the gubernatorial nomination which Rockefeller won, was one of them. Also named was Assembly Speaker Joseph Carlino and Bernard Newman, former Chairman of the New York City Republican Committee.

Senator Mahoney was indignant at the *Life* article and declared it was designed to "smear" Governor Rockefeller. "It is a disservice to its [*Life's*] readers and a calculated effort to damage the Governor's image," said the Senator in wounded tones. "Why, I don't know."

Governor Rockefeller himself declined to be drawn into extended comment about the article. When asked if he had any criticism of the piece, he said only that he thought it was "good journalism."

How much the Governor knew about the extensive corruption in the State Liquor Authority operations is not clear, but it is a detraction from his ordinary powers of observation to suggest that it was unknown to him. The dishonesty cannot be brushed aside as the work of an infiltrator into the political system or a single case breaking out in an otherwise well administered, honest operation. A corrupt way of life existed in the State Liquor Authority and it was spread throughout the system, if there is any validity at all to the dismissals, the testimony, and the indictments that have developed over four or five years. It is uncomplimentary to conclude that Rockefeller's blindness to the situation was a price that had to be paid to a State Republican Chairman to whom the Governor owed so much. If so, payment of the debt left Mr. Rockefeller somewhat bereft of assets that were thought to be

53

ingrained in his character: probity, personal honor, integrity, and the like. At any rate he was spared involvement in the unsavory business by the sequence of events: he was safely elected to a second term before any questions were raised that he might have had to answer.

In his second term, he obtained passage of new legislation affecting bars and package stores, including increased taxes—through what was called a "label use tax"—in direct contradiction to his pledge that no new taxes would be levied. The Governor was sharply critical of the "liquor lobby" and suggested that powerful forces were at work to prevent needed reforms. Rockefeller's critics contended that the repressive liquor laws which he forced through the Legislature would not reduce liquor prices to the consumer, as he contended, and were unrelated to graft prevention. In fact, the real "liquor lobby" was financed by the distillers, and the legislation worked out to their benefit. Liquor prices have not been reduced, confirming his critics' position on the matter and presumably disappointing the Governor, who pledged at the time that lower prices were an aim of the "reform" measures.

New legal provisions did permit opening of more liquor stores under controlled conditions. And a new type of bar-and-grill license now allows an operator, for a fee of up to $1,700 a year, to dispense sp'rits without the necessity of operating a restaurant, too.

Rockefeller named as successor to Morhouse's man Epstein a former investigator for the Federal Bureau of Investigation, D. S. Hostetter. The door to graft and corruption is for the present no longer wide open, but spokesmen for bar owners and package stores insist that reforms in both procedures of the SLA and the law itself are still needed. In particular, owners of small low-gross bars dealing largely in beer sales are incensed. They say that the law requires them to pay the new 2 per cent sales tax on their sales, but point out that they cannot collect sales tax from customers on individual sales of beer at fifteen to twenty-five cents a glass. They contend further that there is a great deal of hidden ownership of bars. Under the law, a proprietor is allowed only one non-restaurant bar license. In practice, however, owners finance other individuals in opening saloons and make private contracts with these dummy proprietors to acquire the income.

The departure of Morhouse as State GOP Chairman put Rockefeller in need of a successor. In 1963 he designated Fred Young, presiding judge of the Court of Claims, to get him the Republican nomination for President in 1964. Mr. Young had other duties as State Chairman, of course, but the party leadership in New York State devoted itself primarily to the objectives of its benefactor, Governor, and man of promise. When the Republican Party nominated Barry Goldwater in 1964, there was the question of what to do about the unsuccessful Mr. Young.

The new presiding judge on the New York Court of Claims was John P. Gualteri who, in two years, had "given new dignity to the court" and accomplished a great deal in doing so. According to the *New York Times,* Judge Gualteri simplified claims procedures, cut judicial red tape, cleared calendars, and brought overdue improvements to a court that, in 1957, had been held up to scorn by an official study commission. As for Mr. Young's service on the court prior to taking over Morhouse's job, the *New York Times* was generous enough to call it "adequate."

When the Goldwater debacle came to its preordained conclusion, Rockefeller found he had an opportunity to put the obliging Mr. Young back on the court. One of the judges on the Court of Claims, the reputation of which Judge Gualteri had sought to improve, was Melvin H.

Osterman, a sixty-two-year-old former Republican leader on Manhattan's West Side. When the state liquor probe disclosed that Mr. Osterman had offered the State Liquor Authority Chairman, Martin Epstein, a $5,000 bribe, and that the latter had agreed to take it, the jurist was ousted from the court. He pleaded guilty to three counts of conspiracy and was sentenced to a year in jail. Fred Young was reappointed to the somewhat sullied sanctity of the court.

The fact that Judge Gualteri, if measured strictly on merit, could be expected to retain his position on the court did not guarantee his security. While it was common knowledge that the Governor wanted to reinstate Young, sooner or later, as presiding judge after he got him back on the Court of Claims, there was some question whether Mr. Rockefeller would quite have the brass to do so. Notwithstanding the confidence with which the Governor sometimes indulges in overt Machiavellian exercises, some Rockefeller admirers felt that putting Young back on the court was a sufficient demonstration of confidence in itself, but that to reinstate him to the position of presiding judge, which entailed removing Gualteri, was stretching the Machiavellian process too far. In doing so, the Governor "will be demeaning an important state tribunal," warned the *Times*.

In February 1966, Rockefeller demeaned it. Gualteri, the stand-in, was demoted, and Mr. Young won his old job back in a blatant political pay-off. Mr. Rockefeller didn't bother about needless candor. He said he was acceding with "utmost reluctance" to Judge Gualteri's request to step down from his $31,500 job and return to service as a trial judge. It was even possible that all of this had been explained to Judge Gualteri in the first place and that the "reluctance" which troubled Mr. Rockefeller was another

56

word for the uneasiness anyone might feel for engineering so transparent a maneuver.

In 1964, as decision time for nominating the GOP candidate for President ran out, Nelson put his machine together, and despite the mounting reaction against him, spoke some foreboding words of wisdom. After Goldwater fanaticism had shown itself in unmistakable strength at a national convention of Young Republicans in San Francisco, Rockefeller said:

. . . as a party and as a people we have been keenly aware of the grave threat posed . . . by international Communism. . . . Many of us have been taking too lightly the growing danger of these same principles from the radical right. . . . Unless Republicans are aroused from inaction . . . the Republican Party is in real danger of subversion by a radical, well financed and highly disciplined minority.

It has become crystal clear that well drilled extremist elements utterly reject these fundamental principles of our heritage. They are embarked on a ruthless effort to take over the party, its platform and its candidates. . . . This cannot be allowed to happen. The [Young Goldwater Republican] tactics are the tactics of totalitarianism. . . . The Birchers and others of the radical right lunatic fringe . . . who successfully engineered this disgraceful subversion [at San Francisco] . . . are the same people who are now moving to subvert the Republican Party itself. . . . They have no concern with and offer no solution for the problems of chronic unemployment, of education and training, of housing, racial injustice and strife.

In the political sphere they offer something equally sinister. . . . it is being seriously proposed . . . that the GOP write off the Negro and other minority groups . . . the industrial states to the South . . . and a scattering of other states.

The transparent purpose behind this plan is to erect political power on the outlawed and immoral base of segregation and

57

to transform the Republican Party. . . . The issue that confronts the Republican Party is the gravest in its history. . . . Its destiny is to save the nation by saving itself.

Not many people will remember that this was Nelson Rockefeller's judgment, framed in a manifesto of his party's direction, in the early Goldwater boom days. This judgment was to be muted, if not silenced, in the grueling primary campaign preceding the GOP national convention.

Nelson married Mrs. Margaretta (Happy) Murphy in May of 1963, some months after Tod Rockefeller had divorced him in Reno, Nevada. He took his new wife along to New Hampshire late in January, 1964, when he opened the fight for the state's convention delegates. There was much talk of their divorce, the remarriage, and Mrs. Rockefeller's obvious pregnancy, and pleasant comments on the equally obvious, radiant happiness they clearly shared. Nelson was called *Rocky* everywhere now. He had said he didn't mind the nickname at all, and it fitted nicely into either a one- or multi-column headline. It also made the front pages of newspapers look like the sports section when it showed up in such screamers as *Rocky Wins Early Rounds,* etc. The style of Rockefeller's folksy-good-guy kind of campaigning in the barbershops and supermarkets was close to a sports-page approach anyway. He received warm receptions, attracted adequate crowds and good-naturedly endured the appraising women who ogled his new wife, but it was all in vain.

Members of the family of Henry Cabot Lodge, then ambassador to South Viet Nam, a couple of lawyers, and a dynamic organizer named Paul Davidson Grindle, of Framingham, Massachusetts, a successful importer of scientific equipment and former New York newspaperman, pulled off an astonishing coup. Lodge, who had not left Viet Nam, won. *Rocky Loses Preliminary Fight!*

Early in 1963, Walter Lippmann, the nation's most widely read and authoritative writer on political and foreign affairs, had written that Nelson's claim on the GOP nomination was so secure that he couldn't possibly prevent it from happening. At national Republican meetings it was simply "assumed" that Rockefeller would be the 1964 nominee.

After the 1964 presidential campaign was well under way, but before Goldwater mesmerized too many otherwise sensible delegates into signing a suicide pact, Lippmann appeared on television with Eric Sevareid in one of his annual "Conversations." This is a passage from that telecast: *

ERIC SEVAREID: Well, what's the trouble with Governor Rockefeller? He's had a lot of Federal government experience, governor of the biggest state in the country. Why hasn't he done better in this campaign?

LIPPMANN: Well, apart from the problems of his private life and his marriage, he was the man best suited by background and training to seize the middle ground for the Republicans, and he hasn't done it. He's conducted a campaign in which he never quite knows whether he's trying to be like Senator Goldwater, or whether he's trying not to be like him. And he's underestimated the American voter, which I think is what the New Hampshire primary shows. And that's probably the most dangerous thing a politician can do. He's tried to get down to a level which is below the level of the people who really make opinion and decide elections. They know he's talking down and they don't want to be talked down to. They *know* he's talking down. They know that Rockefeller isn't as folksy and palsy-walsy as he says he is, and this has been, I think, fatal to this campaign. He's done what a really good politician cannot do—he's stooped to conquer, and of course he's not conquering.

* From *Conversations with Walter Lippmann* (Atlantic-Little Brown, 1965).

59

The charades which followed, with Governor William Scranton, Governor George Romney, Nelson Rockefeller and a shaken host of Republican leaders participating, could not stop the course on which the party delegates were bent. The grinding, exhausting, expensive primaries ran their course and the week of the Republican convention arrived. Rockefeller never had a chance, nor did any other moderate. There was no leadership from Dwight Eisenhower's farm at Gettysburg. There was no one to tell the Republican delegates, who held the power at San Francisco, they were going collectively mad for the moment, and perhaps few would have heard such a voice anyway.

Senator Goldwater alternately captivated and frightened his diminishing following in the late summer and autumn of 1964 while Nelson Rockefeller, in company with millions of fellow Republicans, awaited with despair, silence, or indifference the fate which their party had contrived for itself.

In the end, the Goldwater campaign lost nearly all of the conservative emphasis it had once seemed to possess, and made its pitch directly to the racists and yahoos. President Johnson rose to no glory; in fact he scarcely bothered, except to quiet the country's fears on the Vietnamese war and assure the people that further escalation of the military effort was dangerous and unnecessary. He did not contribute much to Goldwater's defeat, except by being there, calming war fears, still standing in John F. Kennedy's long shadow, waiting for the election returns to come in and banish the ghost with which he had lived.

Nelson Rockefeller now had to do it all over again.

Divorce American Style

3

Just as the public was speculating about the impending divorce of Nelson and Tod Rockefeller, tragedy struck them.

Their twenty-three-year-old son Michael had gone to New Guinea with a Harvard-Peabody project in 1961. He left in April with an expedition headed by Robert Gardner, and accompanied by photographer Eliot Elisofon, and Peter Matthiessen, scholar and author.

Prior to Michael's departure, a fire had broken out in the antiquated Executive Mansion in Albany, and Governor Rockefeller had carried his wife down a ladder from the upper storey living quarters.

Newspapers reported that Tod and Nelson Rockefeller had been occupying *separate suites* and pointedly recalled that the Governor and his wife had not been seen together for quite some time. But not until November 17 of that year (1961) did the public learn officially that the Governor and his wife were planning a divorce. In fact, it was not until January 27, 1962, that Mrs. Rockefeller "reluctantly," as the newspapers reported, agreed to spend the required time in Reno, Nevada, to get the divorce.

News of the breakup of the Rockefeller marriage shared the front pages with reports that Michael was missing in the New Guinea region where the Eilanden River sweeps out into the Arafura Sea, a shark-infested waterway surrounded by swampy shores. Nelson got the cabled news while having lunch with his brother David at Pocantico Hills. It was two days after his separation from Tod had been officially disclosed. By nightfall, he was on the way to New Guinea aboard a jet with his daughter Mary, Michael's twin sister.

Michael and a Dutch anthropologist, Rene Wassing, in company with two tribal boatmen, had attempted to negotiate a river crossing in a catamaran, two thirty-foot canoes lashed together and powered by an outboard motor. En route across the estuary that separated two river villages, the catamaran capsized and the motor was washed out. Twenty-foot tides engulfed the party as the swirling current heaved them, clinging to the craft, out to sea. The boatmen swam to shore to spread the warning and seek help. When help did not come, Michael—buoyed by an empty gas tank and a water can—started to swim for shore, which was by then many miles off. Eight hours later, a Dutch patrol boat rescued Wassing, who had stayed with the waterlogged craft.

A massive search over water and along primitive jungle coastlines was undertaken by the Dutch, but the young man's body was never found. In a rented airplane, Rockefeller and Mary flew at treetop level over vast tropical areas in a heartbreaking search of their own. They remained in Hollandia through the Thanksgiving weekend, hopes dwindling until they were gone.

Mary departed for Manila to join her husband, Lieutenant William Strawbridge, who was stationed there, and Nelson went on to New York. Reporters met him at the airport and the eyes of some filled with tears as he spoke a hushed and poignant soliloquy for his lost adventurous son. They were warm and simple words that revealed some part of the hidden heart of the man and something of the private memory and vision of his son:

"Even as a little boy, he was always aware of people, their feelings, their thoughts. He always loved people and was loved in turn . . . he loved life . . . the beauty of life, of people, of art, and nature."

Nelson Rockefeller went at once to Pocantico Hills where Michael's mother had waited out the agony, and the Governor and his estranged wife were together again for a while in their grief.

Mrs. Rockefeller got her divorce in March of 1962, waiting out her time of residence at a ranch in Nevada. Nelson, after returning from New Guinea, completed his preparations for the upcoming legislative session. Just as Comptroller Arthur Levitt and some of the opposition voices in the political arena had predicted, the state faced a deficit in its 1963–64 budget. As earlier reported, and as required by law, the budget must be balanced. Rockefeller had beaten his opponent, Robert Morgenthau, by 529,000 votes on his record of fiscal stability and a pledge of no new taxes.

Jacob Javits, his Republican running mate for the United States Senate, won by a million votes, leading some of the more insensitive Republicans to suggest that Javits might make a promising candidate for Governor next time around. This kind of thoughtful, if casual, talk was tolerated in Rockefeller circles at the time—after the elections of 1962—when Nelson and his staff could scarcely have cared less about which acceptable Republican succeeded him. *He* was headed for the GOP nomination. After the Goldwater carnival of 1964, however, any mention in Rockefeller circles of Senator Javits' vote-getting strength was bad form.

The Rockefeller staff, and, indeed, politically concerned people throughout the country, watched and measured reaction to Nelson's divorce through the Kennedy year of 1962. Polls showed that Rockefeller's stock dipped sharply after the impending divorce was announced, but a bull market in his candidacy reasserted itself.

In Albany, the Governor signed more than 1,000 bills and vetoed 265 others. He proposed raising automobile license charges and liquor taxes, contending that an increase in "fees" was not a violation of his no-tax promises. The Legislature turned him down on license fees, but gave him his liquor "fee" to help him make up the $100 million deficit.

Rockefeller hit the campaign trail again with a series of speeches that must have kept his press relations aide, Robert McManus, and his principal writer, Hugh Morrow, hard at work. The reaction was good on a tour of the Northwest, even in the dry heat of Goldwater country. He took a hard line against John F. Kennedy and seemed to be far out front of such newcomers as William Scranton of Pennsylvania and George Romney of Michigan. In California, Governor Pat Brown defeated Richard Nixon who, in a final flare-up of temper, backed out of politics for a time. In the spring of 1963, Nelson's fancy turned not only to thoughts of politics, but to love.

There had, naturally, been talk. A short item had appeared in a news magazine which made reference, comprehensible only to those who knew the facts, to a "Mrs. Murphy" and contained a pun on the word "happy."

Dr. James S. Murphy, a microbiologist for the Rockefeller Institute, lived with his lively, splendidly attractive wife in a fine house down the westward slope of the Rockefeller Estate, just off famed old Gory Brook Road. James and Margaretta Murphy, with their four children, had been friends of Nelson's and Tod's, and they had been married fourteen years. Mrs. Murphy was nicknamed Happy, a tribute to her sunny disposition.

Happy Murphy got her divorce in Idaho on April 1, 1963, a year after Tod Rockefeller had got hers, and moved off to a house in Bedford Hills, across county from the Rockefeller barony. Happy had signed away custody of her children, although the separation agreement made provisions for visitation rights. The Idaho judge ordered the records in Happy's case sealed, "in order," press accounts reported, "to protect the children," whose ages ranged from three to twelve. Sealed records probably extended some protection, too, to the fifty-five-year-old governor and the thirty-six-year-old Happy, since they were spared disclosure of very private matters which in more routine divorce cases both unprotected children and adults alike must endure.

Early in May, Helen Logan, the Mount Pleasant town clerk, was summoned from her second floor office above the North Tarrytown National Bank to take a marriage license to the Pocantico Hills home of the Governor's brother Laurance, where the wedding was to take place. There was a mild flutter about the license fee, which no one had immediately on hand, but the matter was resolved. Carl Spad, the Governor's Appointments Secretary, who later replaced Fred Young as State Republican Chairman, was on hand to run small but essential errands. A Rocke feller man never knows where his work will take him.

The wedding ceremony on May 4 was quite private: just a few members of the two families, including Nelson's brother Laurance. The bride wore blue and carried spring flowers. Nelson sported a white carnation on the lapel of his dark blue business suit. A Presbyterian minister, the Reverend M. L. Smith, of the Rockefeller family's Pocantico Hills Union Church, performed the marriage cere-

65

mony, for which he was later admonished by his Hudson River region ministerial body. In its form, however, it was the mildest rebuke of several alternatives open to his fellow clergymen.

Following the nuptials, the couple and members of the wedding party posed for photographs. The bride's mother was quoted as saying she was delighted, and gave a passing bit of sprightly comment on the gala affair. Announcements of the wedding were dispatched to the newspapers by messenger.

The newlyweds flew off to faraway Venezuela for a three-week honeymoon at Nelson's ranch, thence to the Virgin Islands, where the Rockefellers operate a resort hotel. In the course of their idyll, a good deal of hell broke loose back home. Newspapers reported that the New York State Congressional delegation in Washington and Republican political leaders were receiving angry communications and holier-than-thou protests against the marriage from aggrieved citizens. Unquestionably, a good many of these outpourings reflected bitterness against Rockefeller from opportunistic right-wing elements who were less concerned about the marriage than they were about destroying him as a Republican presidential candidate, and doubtless would have been unremittingly against him if he had committed himself to a life of monasticism.

There was a tidal wave of newspaper editorials, supplemented by radio and television commentary. Much of it was pointless twaddle and simply used up space and time, but balanced against the "Good luck, Happy and Rocky" type of cheerful verbiage were critical rebuffs and always—always—there was the printed or spoken question of what all this would mean to Nelson's quest for the presidency.

The anti-Rockefeller wing of the Republican Party

momentarily picked up a friend and supporter it would have preferred to be spared. In Soviet Russia, Premier Khrushchev, no doubt appealing to the virtuous provincial vote in that country, drew a splendidly baroque picture of life among the plutocrats when, in a reference to the Rockefeller-Murphy marriage, he denounced "parasitic capitalists who live a life of luxury, drinking, carousing, and changing wives." The Goldwater movement, taking strength from the gathering momentum, scarcely faltered as the Soviet premier added his unwelcome bulk to the moralistic bandwagon.

Late in September, unaccompanied by Happy, Rockefeller went to Rome for an audience with the Pope, a most unusual development under the circumstances and not entirely free of public relations overtones. But the depressing situation was not measurably changed.

Nelson was encouraged by some sociologists and editorial writers to stand up and fight for the right of divorce and remarriage, to come to grips with the subject in direct terms. It was his marriage to Happy, and not necessarily the break with Tod, that seemed to endanger public support for his candidacy. As the summer wore on, the dialogue continued, to the advantage and comfort of Barry Goldwater. He was the greatest political beneficiary in the United States, with the ultimate exception of Lyndon B. Johnson, of the Rockefeller-Murphy marriage. He had done nothing in September that he hadn't done in May, but he walked off with first prize. Where love had grown, so had his chances to be the great man in the Republican Party. Yet Nelson might have carried it off if insulation from the deeply rooted provincialism of the multitudes, and the courage to face up to a better view of himself, had not focused on a flaw in his character.

Attempts were made to persuade Rockefeller to face

the divorce and remarriage issue in forthright terms, especially after public opinion polls confirmed that he was now a sorry second to the Senator from Arizona. It was an opportunity, one leading authority declared, to cite the archaic divorce law of New York, where a married partner then had to be virtually caught in the act of adultery—or framed in it—to provide grounds for divorce.* There was, he said, an opportunity to assert leadership on the subject, instead of passively permitting rule by public opinion, ill informed and influenced by obscure, unarticulated personal emotions that insist upon a double standard of both values and practice.

John F. Kennedy had faced a similar, if less suddenly invoked, problem as the first Catholic candidate for the presidency since Alfred E. Smith. The issues of divorce and Catholicism were politically similar in that, rationally and factually, neither in itself had any bearing on the capacity, decency, or competence of an honest man. They were similar, too, in the responses they evoke—fear, revulsion, prejudice, masked desire, simple ignorance, and the like. Nelson had said in public only that divorce was a "very personal matter" and that each individual "has to make up his own mind" in passing judgment. This was fair and polite comment but nonetheless evasive.

Kennedy had gone into the heart of the fundamentalist Protestant country in Texas, and stood before an assembly of Baptist clergymen, and discoursed with them—fought them—on ethical and constitutional grounds. When it was over it was significantly clear to the American public, if not to each man of God in Texas, that here was a man deeply and unequivocally committed to the separation of church and state. Kennedy's solid commitment to the prin-

* New York's 179-year-old divorce law was substantially liberalized by the State Legislature in the spring of 1966.

68

ciple of separation was as final and as clear as any Protestant theologian's, but it was firmly rooted in intellectual and constitutional reasoning. It was not a "personal" matter with Kennedy, although it was a religious issue up to that point in Kennedy's campaign. It remained a religious issue afterwards, of course, but largely only among people not responsive to informed discourse.*

In some combination of the deeply moving simplicity revealed when King Edward renounced his throne to marry "the woman I love," and the facts of life pertaining to divorce in the western world, Rockefeller might have been able to reach the American people. True belief and candid explanation have a way of coming through the myth and nonsense that make a populace fear divorce in its leaders, while indulging in it themselves. Perhaps Nelson did not have the ideal divorce to use for articulation of the subject, but the fact remains that, while it bothered the country, there was little expressive evidence from Rockefeller that he understood or that he knew how to allay its feelings.

If Nelson and Happy had gone to the village clerk, got their own license, and proceeded to City Hall for their ceremony—without summoning the clerk to the estate, without pulling the minister of the Rockefeller church into the matter, without, in effect, throwing Rockefeller weight around—a different and more human response might have been evoked. And if some acknowledgment, some understanding and sympathetic concern could have come from the inner heart of the man—something akin to the soft

* Rockefeller himself was conscious of the political similarity between Kennedy's problem with Catholicism and his own divorce and remarriage. In his campaign biography he permitted the author to write: "The primaries [of 1964] were a godsend . . . He [Rockefeller] hoped they would help him demolish prejudices arising from the facts of his marital life as they helped Kennedy destroy the shibboleth that a Catholic could not be elected President."

69

words he spoke to reporters the night he returned from New Guinea—the tide might have been reversed. What a man *feels* is hard, almost impossible, to hold back. What he does not feel cannot, usually, believably be conveyed.

Tod Rockefeller deserved sympathy and understanding; she could not help being the way she was—disinterested in, if not repelled by, politics and political life; a somewhat chill lady, people who like her have said, rather a martinet at times. She could not change substantially, and would doubtless not care to, any more than would Nelson himself. In a different age—today, for example—people like Nelson and Tod might have, in their youth, gone out together, loved, possibly had a love affair, seen early that the factors of attraction were outweighed by the factors of impermanence, and gone—sadly, perhaps, but not traumatically—about their separate ways. But in *their* youth, sheltered and chaperoned, they got married, had five children, and when they were grown, Nelson and Happy met, and after a good many years—eight or nine years, it seems—they divorced and remarried each other. In Happy's case, explanations were harder because the children were younger, but the reaction to their marriage might have been ameliorated.

Public response to old sacrosanct subjects—sex, divorce, birth control, abortion law, the death penalty—has been seething with change as healthy and enlightened viewpoints gained ascendancy, if not general acceptance. The old puritanical moralisms, lacking a strong intellectual basis, were vulnerable to rationality, to conscience, and to precepts of individuality and humanism. Even religious taboos, generally the most rigid and habit-forming of the laws of behavior, were yielding under the questioning of theologians, scholars, and interested laymen. The legislatures of many states and countries were reviewing legal

70

proscriptions of formerly forbidden behavior in response to rising pressure to get the government out of the business of circumscribing and punishing private conduct.

It was perhaps not necessary for Nelson Rockefeller to satisfy America's conscience on the question of his marriage to Happy Murphy, but it might have been wise for him not to ignore those whose sensibilities were affected. He could not expect to evoke understanding, forgiveness, or detachment by retreating from the issue, while now and then suggesting that it was a matter each person had to resolve for himself.

The issue was far more significant to millions of people, though perhaps it shouldn't have been, than it *appeared* to be to Nelson Rockefeller. It was this that allowed his political opposition to exploit his private life to their advantage.

Newspapers, forever exploiting the sensational in the private lives of public men, kept mentioning Rockefeller's divorce, and thus the issue would neither die nor go away.

Too late to do Rockefeller any more harm—since all the harm had been accomplished—a secondary aspect of the remarriage broke into the news again. In the late summer of 1964, legal proceedings instituted by Happy to regain custody of her children opened in the Westchester court at White Plains, where Dr. Murphy and *his* new wife appeared to testify in private, as did Happy herself and supporting witnesses for each side.

All of the principles in the case were tight-lipped when confronted by television cameramen and newsmen, and little information emerged from the hearings to enlighten or titillate the public.

Nevertheless, additional criticism of the former Mrs. Murphy's custody action was given public notice. A Westchester minister, the Reverend Harald E. Bredesen, pastor of the First Reformed Church of Mount Vernon, addressed his parishioners in a sermon that was given prominence in the newspapers. The *New York Daily News* reported that the clergyman had expressed sympathy for Dr. Murphy, "who, having seen his first wife leave him, is now threatened with deprivation of his children. . . . Having left him, [Mrs. Rockefeller] now seeks to take her children with her, thus making his desolation complete. What was his offense? Simply that another man, whose power and prestige were as great as his principle is small, coveted his wife and she coveted him. . . . To have him she was willing to break up her marriage and sign away her children. Now that she has him she wants her children, too. Her desire is quite natural and quite unjust."

True to the taboo against discussion of personal matters, no one in the Rockefeller family, or the Murphy family either for that matter, has ever reported on Nelson's or Happy's reaction to such severe chastisement. They kept their own counsel and let it pass. But an individual with a professional connection to the family was once in a room with Nelson and Happy when some guarded, courteous comment was made on the subject. Each of them, in the drawing room conversation that developed, was saddened by the criticism the other had to endure and each said undefensively that they had done the only proper thing dictated by the circumstances: get married. Implicit in their dialogue was a remembered concern for others who were disturbed by their choice of action, but it was balanced against the only alternative open to them: not to get married. Each found in the other, in knowledge and sureness that was gained, not impulsively but over a long period of time, a capacity for empathy, delight, and love that was not present in their own domestic environments.

People cannot be expected to reject, as a spartan sacri-

72

fice, a course of personal action that is allowable and legal, and that they recognize is, while difficult, essential to their well being. It is highly probable that this is what Nelson meant when he had said divorce was a "personal" matter on which each person must make up his own mind. In the context of their own lives, what Nelson and Happy did was understandable. It was just not a good idea for a man who wanted to be President.

On September 30 the decision of the Westchester court was disclosed. Custody of the children was denied to Happy, and she was directed to return her four-year-old daughter to Dr. Murphy. Her right of visitation was upheld.

Nelson was able to turn his full attention to politics once more.

4

Two Cents for
Mr. Rockefeller

The sweep against the Republican presidential candidate in the 1964 elections decimated Rockefeller's previously Republican legislature, leaving the Governor in control of only minority remnants in both the Assembly and the Senate. He was in serious trouble, with his promised fiscal stability threatened by deficits and that lamentable old pledge of "no new taxes for four years" facing him in the hostile Legislature. As things developed, the lawmakers of the majority Democratic party were so unprepared for victory that they wound up disapproving of each other more than they disapproved of Rockefeller. He used their mutual disenchantment to extraordinary advantage.

When the Legislature convened in January of 1965, Rockefeller had a problem on his hands. Even his home county, Westchester, a bastion of Republicanism since McKinley's time, had been taken by President Johnson and Senator Robert F. Kennedy, who had only lately become a legal resident of the state.

The most dismaying election reversal for Governor Rockefeller was the defeat of a Republican stalwart, Robert Barry, by Richard L. Ottinger in the 25th Congressional District, which embraces the Rockefeller estate, much of Westchester County, and all of the east shore Hudson Valley communities from the New York City line to the northern tip of Putman County. Ottinger, a young and wealthy Harvard lawyer, had made a campaign issue out of the deteriorating Hudson River and charged Rockefeller with aiding the ruination of the region.

Eighty-eight Democrats and sixty Republicans made up the 1965 State Assembly, with a Democrat-controlled Senate of fifty-eight members. Their first job was to get organized, which is a great deal more than a passing phrase. Until certain leadership jobs are filled by a process of election, the Legislature cannot function. And for nearly six weeks it didn't.

Normally each party selects, through conference and caucus, a candidate for majority leader in the Senate and Assembly. The winner in a roll call vote becomes the majority leader, or a kind of *pro tem* president or the legislative leader. All lawmaking functions begin with these mandatory selections, which are determined by majority vote. But in this case two bitterly split Democratic factions could not agree on either a Senate or Assembly candidate for the posts. With the Democrats in the majority, a roll call vote should have made any nominee certain of election, and the session could begin.

New York City's Mayor Wagner wanted two cronies, Anthony Travia and Joseph Zaretzki, in the Assembly and Senate leadership posts. The party regulars, weary of Wagner and eager to present their own legislative program, wanted Stanley Steingut of Brooklyn and Senator Jack E. Bronston of Queens in the top legislative jobs. Day after day, roll calls in the Senate put Bronston within three or four votes of the required majority, but none of Wagner's senatorial delegation would yield his vote to Bronston. In the Assembly, Steingut led by fifty-five to thirty-three among the Democrats, not enough for a majority; the stalemate held.

With the entire state legislative machinery in a state of paralysis, Mayor Wagner ordered his men to hold out, notwithstanding their second best position in the vote count.

Both Democratic Mayor Wagner and Republican Governor Rockefeller were in serious fiscal trouble. It was this common need—plus a few fringe benefits of his own that the Governor had in mind—that caused Wagner and Rockefeller to join forces, break the deadlock, and leave Rockefeller, as head of a defeated party, securely in power.

In addition to the fiscal matters which united Wagner and Rockefeller, they had a common interest in preventing the capture of Democratic Party power by U.S. Senator Robert F. Kennedy, whose strength rested largely among anti-Wagner Democrats. President Johnson was as interested as either Rockefeller or Wagner in keeping party legislative machinery out of Kennedy's hands. So when Wagner's forces in the Legislature were directed to continue the stalemate, even though badly outvoted, it was a case of sharing power with Rockefeller as opposed to permitting Senator Kennedy to usurp it. From Wagner's position, it was better to go halfway with the Republican Governor than nowhere with Kennedy. The political dogfight among the Democrats presented Nelson Rockefeller with a bone of promise.

The leadership positions, besides carrying with them prerogatives and power, are adorned with cash bangles marvelously termed "lulus," pronounced *loo-loos*. This is a delightful corruption of the phrase, *in lieu of*. In the case of committee chairmanships and an array of appointed jobs, the lucky winners get lulus, or real money, *in lieu* of expenses. It is not only the $10,000 per year salary that makes a legislator's job worth while, but the lulus as well. When a stalemate develops, as it did in the 1965 session, one must not be overly impressed with the long list of principles advanced by one side or the other in support of its case. It is the faction which corners the market in lulus that achieves the opportunity to advance whatever principles may have survived the battle.

With Wagner's counsel and legislative aide, Bernard Ruggiero, serving as contact man between the Governor and the Mayor, a remarkable deal was devised. Ruggiero had an open telephone line to Wagner "half the time," one legislator reported. With lulus as the bait, the state territory was cut up. Rival leader Rockefeller was given a free legislative hand in the state, excluding New York City, while Wagner got uncontested control of City territory.

In mid-February, with twenty-six roll calls behind them, the Senators started to vote once again on the leadership election. One after another, the Rockefeller Republicans began voting for Wagner's man, Joseph Zaretzki. He won, of course. Rockefeller had put him into the job which an overwhelming majority of his own Democrats had denied him.

In the Assembly, sixty Republicans joined the thirty-three Wagner Democrats who had held out for Travia, and he won, ninety-three to fifty-five. And that's how the Mayor of New York City and Governor Rockefeller, without a majority in either house, took possession of the State Legislature.

Messrs. Travia and Zaretzki joined the exultant Ruggiero in conveying news of their triumph to that gentle master of the art of political survival, Robert F. Wagner.

The days that followed were an eye-bugging exercise in the execution of legislative authority. Rockefeller wanted a state-wide 2 per cent sales tax, probably the most cruel of all tax levies since the percentage of income spent on taxable items by low-income families is far higher than that expended by more affluent voters. However, as Michael Harrington, author of *The Other America,* has pointed out, the poor have no lobby, and of course the more affluent are getting to be pretty numerous. It is, therefore, not as risky politically, from the numbers point of view, to soak the poor, just as it was once, in Franklin D. Roosevelt's time, proper political practice to soak the rich for essential tax revenues. The analogy is oversimplified here, but the point has validity.

The trouble with the state sales tax was that New York City already had its own sales levy. The sticky little problem was compounded by the fact that New York City probably has more poor and low-income families than the rest of the state combined. However, alternative tax measures were intolerable to Rockefeller, and so he sponsored a plan whereby New York City's sales tax would go up to 5 per cent.

Senator Jack Bronston, the Democrat who lost out to the Rockefeller-Wagner coalition and a legal expert on education law, taxation, and finance, joined with several other legislators to propose to Mr. Rockefeller a tax program designed to ease the burden of those least able to pay.

The corporate franchise tax, which hadn't been increased in twenty years, offered a source of revenue, as did a boost in the state income tax, which could be tailored to provide exemptions to some of the 300,000 low-income families Rockefeller had scooped up in his earlier fiscal improvement program.

Rockefeller scoffed at the alternative proposals, for one thing because he had boasted that he had not increased a single tax on business during his long regime and did not intend to begin now. The ability of corporations to pay a tax increase was not questioned especially, but it was felt to be, among other things, bad psychology; new business might be discouraged from coming into the state, or what was worse, old business might consider moving *out* of the state if there was any trifling with corporate taxes.

Even with the mutual back-scratching between him and Wagner, the Governor very nearly didn't get his sales tax— it was too much for some of the Wagner Democrats to take. Seven hold-out Assemblymen from New York's Harlem and Bedford-Stuyvesant districts felt they could not satisfactorily explain to their low-income and impoverished people an affirmative vote for a 5 per cent sales tax. They declined to go along and the bill remained on the legislative calendar through much of the session. Malcolm Wilson and Nelson Rockefeller are patient fellows, but failure to produce the sales tax bill was a frightening prospect. Travia and Zaretzki were in charge of getting the job done and they were not moving with sufficient dispatch. They were willing enough, but the recalcitrant legislators were demanding some kind of legislation to compensate for the harsh sales tax. They explained this day after day as they joined the Governor in the Executive Chamber each morning to plan the schedule for the day. Mr. Rockefeller allowed the City Democratic leaders to take turns sitting in the Governor's sumptuous chair, which is enough to set a lowly legislator's head spinning with dreams and fancies. It is said that the Governor smiled, as well he might, as Mr. Travia in particular seemed to respond to the thrill of sitting in the great chair while having coffee with Mr. Rockefeller. Mr. Zaretzki, rather a coarse fellow by comparison, was not as cheerful as Mr. Travia, but he enjoyed these cozy little morning get-togethers, too, in his own uncultivated way. The opulent Executive Chamber is a nice quiet place in which to schedule the day's work.

The hold-out legislators from Brooklyn and Harlem, who represented a large section of Negro and Puerto

Rican voters, had no lofty aims and their price for going along with the sales tax was not unduly high. They thought it would be nice if New York would take the lead in increasing the state's minimum wage, for one thing. Remembering the leadership assumed by Mayor Wagner's father, whose name adorned the Wagner Labor Relations Act, they did not seem to feel that they were letting the Mayor down by using leverage to press for a minimum wage of $1.50 an hour. Besides, when you agree to increase the City's sales tax to 5 per cent, you had better do *something* to relieve the pain among those least able to afford the new tax.

With the understanding that the Legislature would later pass a new minimum wage law, the reluctant legislators capitulated and the sales tax was signed into law, dutifully supported by most Rockefeller Republicans and Wagner Democrats. It was estimated that in the first full year, it would produce $585 million in revenues, which would let Nelson go into the gubernatorial race again with his pay-as-you-go, balanced budget record theoretically intact.

When sales tax collections began in August of 1965, the protests against it took visible form in many retail establishments, especially small ones. Cans with coin slots appeared on counters beside cash registers, and on the cans were lettered signs, "Rocky's tax" or "Put pennies for Rocky here." Salesclerks gave the price of merchandise as "ninety-eight cents for us and two cents for Mr. Rockefeller." The practice became so general that the Governor took to issuing defensive statements to remind the electorate periodically how much revenue the tax was producing for state services.

Toward the end of the session, some of the Wagner Democrats became uneasy about the failure of any minimum wage revision bill to come before the Legislature. They queried the Governor, who told them that no such bill had come to him for approval or study. It seemed the bill had become "lost" after it reached Mr. Zaretzki. When confronted, Zaretzki ostentatiously dug it out and put it into the legislative gristmill. In due course it was passed and the Governor vetoed it. He said he was afraid it would hurt business.

The bill was revised to set the starting date for its $1.50 hourly provision further into the future. Rockefeller vetoed that one, too. A third bill reduced the increase and established the minimum wage at $1.40 an hour. It faded away in the closing hours of the session, along with the hopes of the Harlem and Brooklyn legislators.

One of the legislative losers, Jack Bronston, pointed to —and handed out copies of—a twelve-page critical summary he had prepared and circulated, at his own expense, prior to the 1965 session. It was largely an analysis of Rockefeller's fiscal policies and might have made an impression on the legislature, as it was doubtless intended to do, except for the fact that the 1965 session was not a truly deliberative body so much as it was an automated production factory. Rockefeller was on hand as the overseer and owner, with Malcolm Wilson as a kind of general manager. Travia and Zaretzki were the division vice presidents, and Wagner was the absentee investor, with Bernard Ruggiero serving as visiting troubleshooter to see that the Mayor's percentage of return was commensurate with the programmed input.

It does not seem, on balance, that Wagner got much, although what he did get was enormously important at the time. At what may turn out to be a dreadful cost to the city in the long run, he picked up $256 million a year in new borrowing power obligingly provided by the State Legislature, thus enabling *him* to claim a "balanced" budget, which the *New York Times* said was clearly "bogus."

Like the state, New York City is required by law to balance its budget. Nevertheless, after John Lindsay was elected Mayor, he declared he found the City on the edge of bankruptcy and said he had the feeling his job would be that of a trustee in receivership. Wagner was hurt by such a suggestion and retorted that the City was in relatively good shape, which no one who could read or add believed for a moment.

Estimates of the budgetary gap between New York City revenue and expenditures for the fiscal year 1966 settled at around a half billion dollars. In an extraordinarily somber appraisal of the city's critical financial condition, the *Times* on November 12, 1965, said:

Although the emergency is the end-result of an accumulation of age-old defects in city management, it is possible to pinpoint its recent worsening almost to the stroke of the clock. The bell tolled for bankruptcy on May 13, 1965, when Mayor Wagner in his annual budget message said: "The best tax is no tax. A good loan is better than a bad tax."

This policy started the city down a toboggan slide in which any claim to a "balanced" budget, as required by law, was bogus. It was based on bond-issue borrowing of $256 million a year for which collateral itself was strictly a gamble: state-wide voter approval, in a referendum next year, of a constitutional amendment increasing the legal rate of taxation on city real estate.

Governor Rockefeller, having given Mayor Wagner territorial rights to the City in return for legislative controls he could not have otherwise exercised, quite literally signed the city into a fiscal morass when he signed the bill

82

putting a prior mortgage on the city's future income—if it gets it.

So much for the benefits that accrued to Mayor Wagner from his union with Nelson Rockefeller.

It is an ironic fact that Rockefeller's exploitation of the factional struggle among the Democrats produced, along with damaging results, some good and necessary bills. Legislation which the Republican-dominated Legislature had consistently rejected for years was passed. It was an extraordinary situation in which Rockefeller could credit his outnumbered Republican administration, and himself, for adopting measures normally distasteful to the GOP. At the same time, Democrats could be blamed, since they were in the majority, for legislation which Rockefeller didn't want passed. It was a virtuoso performance.

The death penalty was finally repealed. Birth control restrictions were liberalized, thus pleasing people who care about both life and death. These achievements were possible primarily because even as normal pressures in favor of legislative accomplishment were not functioning fully, neither were the pressures against it.

It is on fiscal matters, in which Rockefeller publicly takes personal pride, that a severe indictment of the Governor has been made. There are a good many legislators and political leaders who say that Rockefeller has broken the law—violated the state's own constitution—by involving private investment agencies and private profit in the affairs of state government. They contend that he has committed the taxpayers to spend hundreds of millions of dollars over a period of years by establishing private authorities to raise money, at high cost, that legally requires publicly approved bond issues—and that does not show on the balance sheet. Senator Bronston's published summary,

The Great Hoax, sets forth this brief, although the Republican readers will doubtless want to make allowances for what they may suspect is a partisan viewpoint.

The good and the evil of the 1965 legislative session were, as the *New York Times* declared, the work of both major political parties. But in assessing Nelson Rockefeller's contribution, it must be remembered that, while the Democrats had the majority, he—with Wagner's eager help —engineered and supervised the show.

Con Ed's Big Con Job

5

"The Consolidated Gas Co. of New York is notoriously unpopular and conspicuously slack in cultivating the goodwill of the public . . . " *

Fortune Magazine,
July 1935

"Consolidated Edison has developed the most efficient, high-powered lobby in the city and state. It is a lobby that never fails. It is a lobby whose demands grow greater and greater. But despite frequent public protest, it is a lobby toward which public officials and political leaders have usually been receptive." **

New York Post,
April 11, 1961

The two editorial judgments that head this chapter raise the question of how a public utility, notorious for its inability to cultivate the goodwill of the public, can develop a never-failing lobby able to impose its will on public officials, political leaders, and—most of the time—on state and federal regulatory agencies as well.

One answer to the question is: money. Another, which is very nearly the same answer, is that the Rockefellers have been quite helpful.

* Consolidated Gas Co., founded in 1823, through mergers became the Consolidated Edison Company in 1936.
** The author of this quotation, from the opening paragraphs of a series of articles entitled "The Lobby That Never Loses," is Arthur Massolo, a New York Post writer who subsequently went to work for Nelson Rockefeller as an associate of Carl Spad, now GOP State Chairman.

Con Ed produces and distributes electricity, gas, and steam in the populous metropolitan New York and lower Hudson Valley area. Among U.S. utilities it ranks first in assets (well over $3 billion) and second in revenues, which are edging toward $1 billion a year.

In 1884, seven gas companies in Manhattan merged to form the Consolidated Gas Company of New York. Other mergers followed; in 1930, the New York Steam Corporation joined the system. Consolidated Edison brought the New York Edison Company, which was Thomas A. Edison's legacy, together with the steam and gas operations to form the great utility monopoly.

Three generations of the Rockefeller family have made money out of this utility. William Rockefeller, John D.'s brother, was a trustee of Consolidated Gas Company from 1891 until his death in 1922, and was the guiding hand behind many of the mergers and expansion programs. William's son, Percy, replaced his father and served from 1922 until he died in 1934.

Rockefeller Center became the largest customer of the New York Steam Company in the 1930s.

In 1944, the Governor's father, John D. Rockefeller, Jr., sold some of the family's land in Westchester to Consolidated Edison to allow the utility to expand in the county.

The Rockefeller Foundation, launched in 1913 with holdings originally owned by John D., Sr., has held shares in Consolidated Edison in amounts up to $2.6 million.

David Rockefeller, the Governor's brother, is president of the Chase Manhattan Bank, which for years has supplied credit to Con Ed.

After Nelson was elected governor, he was required to list the names of corporations in which he held investments in excess of $10,000. He listed Consolidated Edison, although how much "in excess of" $10,000 he has in the company is not known.

The foregoing digest of the Rockefeller financial tie-in to the Consolidated Edison Company is incomplete, but it is set down here as a possible clue to the Governor's support of a massive hydroelectric plant operation that may despoil for all time a magnificent Hudson River scenic area. It may also disturb the ecology of the region in other dangerous ways. Without understanding the economic factors that relate the Governor and his family to the corporate interests of Consolidated Edison, Rockefeller's assistance to the utility cannot be explained.

In the spring of 1963, a small weekly newspaper in Goshen, New York, a village of three thousand people, printed a paid public notice to the effect that Con Ed proposed constructing a $161 million hydroelectric pump storage about seventeen miles to the east: on the side of Storm King Mountain at Cornwall. This was the first official disclosure of the power project. No such public notice, foes of the project have charged, was published in Putnam and Westchester counties, through which overhead high tension lines would be strung. This omission has been cited in a legal brief as a violation of a law requiring that notice be "published in the county or counties in which the project or any part thereof or the lands affected thereby are situated." The quoted section of the passage is from the Federal Power Act, under which Con Ed was seeking a license from the Federal Power Commission to get on with the project.

Since 1963, three and perhaps four other electric utility corporations have made studies with the intention of installing additional hydroelectric complexes in the mountainous, or "Rhine" section, of the Hudson highlands, according to lawyers who have been engaged by citizens and conservationist groups to protect the Hudson River Valley against Con Ed.

What's wrong with having power plants along the Hudson? Everyone concedes that the expansion of power-producing facilities is essential to economic growth. If Governor Rockefeller feels it is all right to allow Con Ed and a half dozen other utility monopolies to erect hydroelectric complexes along a river running through his state, what's wrong with it? It is the genuine concern of any Governor of any state to encourage economic growth, more jobs, new tax revenues and a more abundant life for all. What, then, is all the fuss about?

The answer lies in the fact that the experience of the last hundred and fifty years, and in particular the past twenty years, guarantees the continued ruination of a vast area unless projects such as Con Ed's are outlawed.

The Hudson River is an estuary opening into New York Harbor and extending to Albany, where it is joined by the Mohawk, thence northward to land west of Lake Champlain, where it has its first discernible origins in a tiny mountain rivulet across which a child can step. For more than three hundred miles it sluices southward; in confluence with the Mohawk at Albany, it emerges into a low valley that rises to an inspiring gorge in the Hudson highlands, widening into a great zee, with hundreds of coves and inlets along its banks, at Tomkins Cove across from Peekskill. It is at its widest—three to three-and-one-half miles—at several points between Haverstraw and Tarrytown, where the great Tappan Zee Bridge of the New York State Thruway connects Rockland and Westchester counties.

A few miles north of Albany lies the city of Troy, where pollution from upstream joins with that of the city itself to create a cesspool of sewage and wastes that is multiplied by the effluence pouring down the Mohawk from the industrial cities of Schenectady, Utica, Syracuse, and scores of smaller towns.

Southward, hundreds of industrial plants, from one-family operations to giant manufacturing and chemical industries, join with villages and towns in using the Hudson as a gigantic, beautiful sewer. Some communities dump their entire output of excrement and commercial pollution into the river, through what the State Health Department calls "outfalls," or into small tributaries connecting with the Hudson. Virtually all the communities and industries are violating the law, and have been doing so, in many instances, for twenty to forty years. Industry has chosen to locate along the estuary in many cases simply because it provided, through lack of enforceable laws, free sewage outlet—free of cost and free of responsibility. Municipalities chose to run their effluence into the river because they could not afford, or would not agree, to build filter and treatment plants. Those that did build them soon found their facilities inadequate for the type and volume of wastes that developed with expansion and increased population. The solution to the absence of, or lack of, treatment facilities was a simple one: pollution was deflected into the great river.

The New York Central Railroad runs at water level along the east bank of the Hudson. Freight lines parallel parts of the west bank, thus sealing off access to the river or making it difficult and hazardous to reach except where overhead bridges or underpasses have been built. Construction of railroad tracks at the river's edge effectively prevented the development of river-oriented towns, which turned their backs on the waterway after the nineteenth century and faced onto the proliferation of roads and high-

89

ways. For mile after mile along the riverside the land is derelict and blighted, a sickening succession of rotting piers and abandoned buildings, strewn junk, oil-encrusted banks, and scum-larded riprap walls.

Yet the river is deep and swift, and the swing of the tides and the curative power of saline water from the sea plus the restorative dynamism of oxygen has not yet permitted the destruction of all marine life. That threat, though, is a real one: the great sturgeon which once reflected silver, shimmering vitality as they broke the surface, are virtually gone, and the Hudson shad, a prized delicacy that graced thousands of dining tables in the region until about 1950, are now diminished in number and often inedible because they are ingested with oil. One by one, shad fishermen have taken in their nets, and the trucks which each spring went from dock to dock, collecting iced boxes of freshly caught shad, do not make their runs any more.

Below the topsoil on land where housing developments have sprung up in Westchester and Rockland County river towns, builders still find a compressed layer of crustacean whiteness—sometimes fourteen to eighteen inches thick— a modern archeological testament to the vast tonnage of shellfish on which life along the valley was nourished. To eat a clam or crab from the Hudson today, if one can be found, is an invitation to hepatitis or at best a grouchy stomach.

Remaining areas of open waterfront still look out on vistas of grandeur, with whitecaps dancing up to meet lowering mists against a backdrop of palisade walls or second-growth forested hills. There are breaks of awesome beauty spotted between the dumps and the slime of a century of wreckage and ruin, and in these—and along points reclaimed as parks—people still risk a swim or sit on the rocks and dangle a crab line into the water. In back eddies, removed from the swifter channel, pollution is at times nominal and use of the river, without excessive danger to health, is permissible. But save for boating and sporadic fishing, and of course for looking at, where the views remain open, the great river is lost today to the people.

Executives of the Consolidated Edison Company took the position that the river was so far gone, and its shores so blighted that anything they wanted to do could only improve it. With rock fill gouged from Storm King mountain, into which its hydroelectric plant is to be built, Con Ed has promised to build a river-edge park for the town of Cornwall, in addition to which the installation would multiply by ten times present tax revenues of the community. The utility has argued that the demolition of rotted piers and ramshackle abandoned buildings, and their replacement by a park, would esthetically improve that specific area. The promise of this largesse, which enables Con Ed to dispose easily of the rock to be cut from the mountainside, has quite naturally won from many people in the local area acquiescence to the project.

There are larger and dangerous considerations, however, which rest in the nature of a pumped storage plant in that location.

Storm King Mountain is fifty miles north of New York City, which would be the principal market for the power to be produced there. Con Ed has never been too precise, nor has the Federal Power Commission which licensed the project, about the volume of electricity to be developed. Its testimony includes estimates from 1.8 million kilowatts up to 4 million.

The plan calls for the disembowelment of the east face of the great mountain, in which generators would be installed. Water from the Hudson would be pumped up a two-mile conduit tunnel, forty feet wide, and twelve billion gallons of it would be stored in a great reservoir swaying between Mount Misery and White Horse peaks. Water would be pushed to the top of the mountain in the off-peak hours, then during the period of heavy demand in New York City, it would run back down the tunnel, turn the generators, and spill back into the Hudson.

An astonishing feature of the Storm King operation is that Consolidated Edison plants in New York City must supply the power to run it. The Cornwall plant, in terms of measured power, will *consume* three kilowatts for every two it produces. It will eat up 33 per cent more power each day than it puts out.

This single uncontested fact—uncontested either by Con Ed or the Federal Power Commission—made ill-informed at best, or a liar at worst, out of anyone who told the public that the Storm King plant would add to total power production capacity. In his bizarre defense of the Con Ed project, Governor Rockefeller was on the worst side of the case.

To the layman, the fact that the plant would produce less power than it used, opened up the question of why Con Ed would *want* to spend $161 million on such a facility. Con Ed contended that the so-called "pumped storage" hydroelectric plant gave it a daily opportunity to store power production capacity during the night, when consumption was low, and use it in the high-consumption daytime periods in New York City. Ordinarily, electricity must be consumed as it is produced, but by having eight billion gallons of water in mountaintop reservoirs, it is possible, by opening the sluice gates, to increase power production quickly. Thus, while it is not possible to store electricity, the hydroelectric plant stored the capacity to manufacture it instantly.

There were three other reasons why Con Ed wanted the Cornwall plant. First, it had spent a great deal of money on this project area, long before the FPC gave it permission—which the courts withdrew—to go ahead with construction. The only way Con Ed could justify its expenditures, which may have amounted to several million dollars, was to complete the project. With the Governor in its corner and certain of FPC approval, which was regarded as a mere formality, the public utility saw no problem in getting overcommitted. The FPC and Con Ed, it will be remembered, had a history of never losing a case—which was why Laurance Rockefeller, for example, said protests were useless.

Second, Con Ed wanted to serve as a power broker in the Northeast. With a pumped storage plant able to become operable in a matter of minutes, and with a sufficient variety of electricity-producing facilities, money can be made by a utility which has stored power on hand. This does not especially serve customers in the Con Ed area, but rather opens up the possibility of lucrative sales to other power companies.

Third, there is the matter of corporate psychology. In a combat with the people, the corporation likes to win; so do the people, for that matter. But virtually all of the weapons in such a combat are in the hands of the public utility. It is a matter of both policy and competitive reflex to make use of these mechanisms. Once a great deal of money and engineering time have been spent planning and proposing a project, voluntary withdrawal for any reason is improbable. The lobby has spent money, commitments have been made, government officials have been persuaded, and pride has become involved. When things have gone this far, it is hard to reverse oneself—as Governor Rockefeller, among others, knows so well.

Since the power to run Storm King must be generated in the city, Con Ed was caught in another deception with its claim that the Cornwall plant would reduce city air pollution—much of which is caused by Con Ed in the first place. For a time the public was allowed to entertain the hope that the city's plants, producing power with coal and oil as fuels, would be relieved of duplicating power generated fifty miles away. Alas, such was not the case. In fact, city plants will have to work harder and longer simply to keep the Storm King plant functioning.

For what it is worth, residents of New York City can look forward to one esthetic benefit arising from the Cornwall operation. City power plants will be working largely in the nighttime and predawn hours generating power needed to pump water from the Hudson River into the mountaintop reservoirs. Belching smokestacks will not be seen at night. Air pollution index readings are not so frightening if the pollution-producing causes are not constantly visible. Peak demands for power in New York City occur, naturally, in the daytime hours. In these periods, power produced by letting water out of the Storm King reservoirs would cushion peak power requirements until, in the dark of night, local plants could begin generating the current to fill up the reservoirs again.

When Con Ed advanced the argument that its Storm King operation would reduce air pollution, it was palpably false. After a time, the argument was not used again. Unfortunately, neither Governor Rockefeller nor the Federal Power Commission provided much enlightenment on the air-pollution or other negative aspects of the Cornwall project.

Upriver from the proposed Storm King plant, New York City has its Chelsea pumping station, which had been built when drought and leakage in the City water system

94

had caused a grave shortage in the late 1950s. It was abandoned and allowed to fall into disuse once melting snow and a period of rain eased the water shortage. This type of crash construction of facilities to cope with city problems, and the abandonment of them upon the passing of an immediate crisis, has been a characteristic of long-range planning in New York City.

In 1965, when a four-year drought reduced reservoir supplies to less than one fourth of capacity, another crash project was authorized to repair and reinstitute the Chelsea station to pump water from the Hudson.

The Con Ed plant at Storm King would pose a grave threat to the Chelsea plan. The Hudson River, aside from being heavily polluted, is brackish and saline off the top when, at ebb tide, the heavier salt water lies beneath it. But if Con Ed was going to be pulling eight billion gallons out of the river and dumping it back, twice a day turbu lence would be certain to mix tidal salt water with fresh water and make the Chelsea intake supply unusable.

Another danger in Con Ed's plans, and from an ecological standpoint perhaps the most far-reaching one, would be the effect of the exchange of eight billion gallons of water on marine life in the river. While much of this life has already withered under the filth and neglect of the river, some commercially important fish resources remain.

Stripers, as fishermen call the striped bass which abound in the sea from New England to New Jersey, spawn in the Hudson and are heavily concentrated in the Storm King area. Larvae are highly vulnerable, according to marine biologists, to any disruption of their natural environment. If drawn up into the Con Ed conduits, survival would be impossible. Yet Con Ed declared, in the testimony of its witness before a Federal Power Commission hearing, that no harm would come to the fish. The

400,000 fishermen in the Northeast who catch striped bass, and who make it an industry estimated at $40 million annually, had nothing to worry about, Con Ed testified. There were good reasons why this testimony, which the FPC never questioned, was unbelievable.

First, the Con Ed witness, Dr. Alfred Perlmutter, was a former employee of the State Conservation Department. At the time of his FPC testimony he was an associate professor at New York University—and a consultant for Con Ed. He admitted that the most recent study, on which his optimistic outlook for the safety of the fish at Storm King, was made in 1938. No other marine biologists were present to contradict his testimony. But when the substance of Dr. Perlmutter's conclusions became known, several organizations interested in protecting fish life in the Hudson joined in seeking further hearings before the FPC. They wanted to introduce testimony to the effect that the striped bass spawning grounds *would be* directly endangered by the Storm King power plant.

The FPC flatly declined to engage in further discussions about the fish matter, so it remained for the New York state legislative hearings to bring out the truth. It developed that a later study, completed in 1956, contradicted Con Ed's testimony. The study was made by two biologists, Warren Rathjen and Lewis Miller, and findings were published by the State Conservation Department itself.*

Did Dr. Perlmutter or Consolidated Edison know of the 1956 findings, the biologists were asked? Yes, they did. "In fact," said one of them, "Perlmutter hired us." When the FPC granted the Storm King license to Con Ed, Commissioner Charles Ross deplored "testimony about which serious doubts have arisen."

Secondly, Con Ed's reputation for honest reporting

* *Sports Illustrated,* April 6, 1965.

96

had been besmirched in the past, and the credibility of any witness is, normally, a factor in decisions resulting from it. Not, however, before the Federal Power Commission, which has other fish to fry.

Consolidated Edison operates a nuclear power plant at Indian Point, on the east Hudson shore, near Montrose, New York. It was built in the 1950s without organized opposition from conservationists, who later regretted their nonresistance. The Indian Point plant, contrary to irrational fears of the uninformed, causes no hazards from radiation or anything else except heat. Water is drawn from the river to cool reactors and discharged back into the river. Weirs are supposed to protect fish from being sucked into the intakes.

As hearings on the plant at Storm King disclosed, Con Ed was not averse to offering untruthful testimony. Con Ed and the New York State Conservation Department, headed by Commissioner Harold Wilm, publicly denied that fish had been killed at Indian Point. There was talk of "mountains" of dead fish, reportedly seen by the citizens of Montrose and Buchanan, communities near the Con Ed nuclear plant. But curious students of wild life who went to look were chased off by armed guards. Testimony on this matter before the hearings of the FPC, which showed little interest in the marine life issue anyway, was not conclusive.

In November, 1965, after the transcripts of the FPC licensing hearings had been released, it was clear from the text that the Con Ed fish story did not get full and truthful attention. It was also clear, as the Con Ed case became more understood in its details, that the Federal Power Commission was going to grant a license to build the Storm King project. But in doing so, it would have to reject as invalid, or beyond the range of its concern, virtually all of the issues raised against the plant.

One ominous effect of the plant was cited by Leopold C. Rothschild, a New York lawyer who had become president of the Scenic Hudson Preservation Conference, an organization with supporters from all over the United States, which had been formed for the explicit purpose of trying to save the Hudson Valley from desecration and industrialization.

Mr. Rothschild and his professional aide, Rod Vandivert, a specialist in conservation public relations, picked the brains of hydraulic engineers, dam designers, and other specialists and confirmed their suspicions that the Con Ed project carried with it an appalling danger to water resources of the area. Others analyzed the project in terms of its necessity, costs, esthetics, ecological damage, acquisition of land for power lines, and so on. When State Senator Robert Watson Pomeroy of Dutchess County, New York, Chairman of the Joint Legislative Committee on Natural Resources, called for public hearings, they were all ready.

Senator Pomeroy is a cultivated, soft-spoken, died-in-the-wool Republican of rigid political outlook who loves the Hudson Valley as Henry Thoreau loved Walden. The Joint Legislative Committee was set up by the 1964 State Legislature to make a general study relating to the protection of natural resources in New York. It was not intended to concentrate exclusively on the Con Ed project, but that's about all it did. Mr. Pomeroy and his associates on the bipartisan committee were not prepared for the outcry that sounded when they opened two days of public hearings at Bear Mountain Inn on November 19–20.

Clusters of Con Ed men, together with representatives of several labor unions who understandably wanted construction jobs at the power plant, appeared wearing bright-colored lapel signs bearing the offensive threat, "Dig We Will," a parody of the public relations message, "Dig

We Must—For a Growing New York," which appears around street excavations. They were outnumbered perhaps twenty-to-one by people enraged at the Con Ed proposal.

The magnitude and destructive aspects of the Con Ed project became increasingly apparent as Pomeroy heard a parade of witnesses from a score of communities threatened with overhead power lines—conservationists, housewives, scientists, fishermen, schoolteachers, bird watchers, and just people.

Some new facts came to light. Con Ed would have to purchase the main fresh water reservoir owned by the village of Cornwall and flood it each night with saline, polluted water from the Hudson. Cornwall, despite all the money it would get in taxes from Con Ed, would be left without water. Its recourse was to tap New York City's Catskill Aqueduct, diminishing a dwindling supply that was further endangered by the prolonged drought.

Cornwall might not have given up its excellent fresh water supply if it had not been, as *The Nation* put it, "bullied into doing so by the Federal Power Commission." Also, Governor Rockefeller had come to the rescue of Con Ed. Under the law, no New York community had any right to tap into New York City's Catskill water aqueduct. But in 1963, Rockefeller had hurried through the legislature a bill permitting such a privilege—one that has thus far been assumed exclusively by Cornwall.

Throughout the FPC hearings, its own public relations campaign, and through witnesses before the Pomeroy hearings, Consolidated Edison presented seemingly incontrovertible charts and data showing the necessity for the Storm King plant, the precise location of overhead high tension towers, scale models showing the topographical design and graphs of peak loads, output, and so on. At the FPC hearings, little refutation of this type of testimony was offered; not many witnesses are readily available with complete knowledge of power plant production to testify against an electric utility.

Alexander Lurkis is a retired chief engineer of the New York City Bureau of Gas & Electricity, who had also been a consultant and engineer in power plant installations. He had had occasion to deal directly with Consolidated Edison in New York City, had familiarized himself with the FPC hearings, and was convinced Con Ed was wrong. But FPC had not heard the testimony of Mr. Lurkis —nobody was very interested in his reports until the Pomeroy hearings came along. But he arrived at Bear Mountain with an array of graphs, charts, and columns of figures no less impressive than those of the Dig-We-Wills.

Mr. Lurkis implied that Con Ed was embarked on a con job. He presented detailed proposals for using gas turbine power production facilities *in the city* in which power was to be consumed. He cited as incorrect and inaccurate Con Ed's own projections for future peak power requirements and its means for coping with them. He claimed that other types of power generating equipment, located in the city, would save customers and ratepayers $132 million in capital expenditures. He showed further, and the FPC chairman subsequently seemed to agree with him, that nuclear generated power—not hydroelectric power—was around the corner for everybody. In fact, Mr. Lurkis said, hydroelectric power such as that proposed at Storm King would be all but obsolescent at the time of installation.

It began to appear from this evidence that Con Ed did not really need the hydroelectric plant at Storm King, regardless of the merits of the conservation issue, the threat to marine life, and damage to a vast area from overhead power lines. In the principal arena of FPC jurisdiction, the question of whether or not the Storm King plant was a true public necessity had not even been questioned. The obliging assistance of Governor Rockefeller, with some oblique but significant help from his brother Laurance, plus the self-serving cooperation of the village of Cornwall, were less excusable in the wake of reasonable doubt about the plant's essentiality.

Robert Boyle, an associate editor of *Sports Illustrated,* testified that he had seen photographs of a half acre of dead striped bass, piled five feet high at the Indian Point power plant dump. He said the State Conservation Department, charged with responsibility for protecting marine life and prosecuting people who destroyed it, was guilty of suppressing facts in the case.

Commissioner Wilm, faithful to the unity presented by officials of the Rockefeller Administration, denied that there had been a loss of fish at Indian Point, although photographs of the extensive slaughter were in the Albany office of the State Conservation Department. Prints of the photographs on file at the Department's Poughkeepsie office were ordered sent to Albany, where they were kept from prying eyes—as part of the State of New York's operations for the protection of Consolidated Edison. It was the careful hush-up of this scandal, with the state running interference for the public utility against which it should have taken punitive action, that kept the story of fish destruction from being fully corroborated at the Pomeroy hearings.

Nevertheless, Mr. Boyle, an angry and persistent journalist, finally obtained the photographs and published them in *Sports Illustrated,* after which the press carried reports that the State Conservation Department "admitted" some fish were killed at Indian Point, but not many. Finally,

101

Senator Pomeroy himself demanded to see the pictures and Commissioner Wilm sent two of them to his house.

"They were fairy sizable fish kills," said Mr. Pomeroy. A courteous man, Senator Pomeroy did not pass judgment on the diligence with which the Conservation Department had gone about its task of ferreting out the destroyers of the state's fish resources. However, in defense of the hapless Mr. Wilm of the State Conservation Department, it must be understood that Con Ed had a protector in Governor Rockefeller, and subordinate commissioners do not routinely go about prosecuting the Governor's friends.

In any case, the Conservation Department and Con Ed relieved each other of responsibility. Con Ed was willing to allow the Atomic Energy Commission, which had to approve the Indian Point plant, to take the blame for the fish kill. The Conservation Department called the death of the fish "an act of God," inferentially decorating Con Ed with the highest accolade ever pinned on a lobby.

Commissioner Wilm, when criticized for going along with Rockefeller on the Storm King project, at no time questioned or admitted the continuing threat to aquatic life. To the Governor's expressed regret, however, Mr. Wilm later resigned as protector of living things to engage in research and teaching, a field which leaves him free of the demanding job of serving as watch-dog over the march of corporate progress along the Hudson River.

No one can ever know for sure the tonnage of striped bass slaughtered at Indian Point. The cause of the carnage seems to be heat. Scalding water, heated as it cools the reactors, elevates the temperature of the river, and the stripers, in a lemming-like response that runs contrary to the good sense normally prevailing in nature, swim toward the warmth and die. It is said that Con Ed has "cured" this condition but on the basis of past experience—and the

earlier denials that it ever happened in the first place—
conservationists and wild life authorities are not comforted. They were even less consoled when the *New York
Times,* just prior to the November elections of 1965, disclosed that Consolidated Edison would double the size of
its Indian Point nuclear plant. The Gannett newspapers,
a Westchester chain which unfailingly supports Nelson
Rockefeller, somehow did not publish the story but within
a day or two printed their own account, which quoted
Con Edison as denying expansion plans at Indian Point.
The protective Westchester papers were proved inaccurate
when Con Ed itself made a subsequent formal announcement, confirming the *Times* story and elaborating on the
details.

With respect to the threatened destruction of the striped
bass spawning grounds at Storm King, Con Ed "experts"
appeared at Bear Moutain to give assurances that screens
and specially designed technological devices would leave
larvae unharmed.

The striped bass issue, because of the importance of
this species of fish to the whole Northeast, cannot be
silenced. The U.S. Fish and Wildlife Service was ordered
to look into the problem—which it failed to do, preferring
to let Con Ed and the State do the job and, possibly, pass
judgment on the merits of the report. Ichthyological geno-
cide, as a concomitant of a power plant project, is not
a concern of the FPC, which has a mandate to help the
killers, not the protectors. As one impassioned witness
said in addressing the Pomeroy Committee:

"You will not hear the cry of the dying fish. But hear
me."

A burly but articulate labor leader, pleading with the
Committee to support the Con Ed project, declared that
"the butterfly catchers and the bird watchers are more

interested in fish than in people." His remark drew peals of explosive laughter from the Con Ed Dig-We-Will contingent, who seemed pleased to have the opponents of the project classified at last.

The testimony on the striped bass problem did succeed in evoking what, to Con Ed, must have seemed like a constructive response. The utility notified Governor Rockefeller that it was willing to spend $150,000 for a three-year study to determine the effect of its hydroelectric plant on fish life.

Governor Rockefeller praised Consolidated Edison in a public pronouncement. Assemblyman Daniel Kelly from Manhattan, who might not be expected to care what happened fifty miles north of his district, made public a letter to the Governor in which he said that it would be "establishing an unethical principle" to allow Con Ed to conduct and pay for its own investigation.

"I can't understand his logic," said Rockefeller, referring to Kelly's letter. "To me it is highly laudable for a private organization to provide a study to determine if what he proposes to do might be detrimental. I think they would be delinquent if they did not do it. I can't understand it."

Mr. Rockefeller seemed quite sincere in his inability to understand objections to Con Ed's offer to pay for the fish study. Hadn't Rockefeller enterprises invariably undertaken studies before making decisions on capital investments? He seemed as oblivious to any conflict of interest or possible mixed motive as he must have been when he gave Judson Morhouse a comfortable little salary on the State Thruway Authority and allowed him to roam around in the State Liquor Authority.

Even to take Mr. Rockefeller's own favorable view of the fish survey, as proposed by Con Ed, a significant question remained to be answered: What would happen if, at the end of three years, the study showed conclusively that the hydroelectric plant would indeed destroy the striped bass spawning grounds forever and ruin the industry? Would the plant be torn down? Or, in the event construction was incomplete, would the project be halted? And what provisions would be made for restoring the clawed-up mountain or undoing damage done by blasting and bulldozers? What would be Con Ed's alternative "highly laudable" proposal?

Two final revelations at the only public hearings of the Joint Legislative Committee produced additional doubts about both the technology and safety of Con Ed's engineering, and the necessity for the project in the first place. Testimony relating to safety of the reservoirs, which had received little emphasis and no press attention in the FPC hearings, was now made in public for the first time. It presented a chilling prospect, as understated in the Pomeroy Committee's report.*

. . . . Testimony was presented . . . that the proposed Con Ed dam does not meet the minimum safety requirements of U.S. Army Corps of Engineers. . . . Five dams would be constructed to impound 12 billion gallons of water. The natural flow of any dam breakage would, in four cases, be through inhabited areas of Cornwall. The fifth dam is poised over Route 9W, a main highway on the west shore. . . . So long as any doubt exists as to the safety of a dam, its construction should be delayed, particularly when the natural flow of any breakage would so greatly endanger lives and property.

A total of 107 witnesses appeared before the Pomeroy Committee. The thrust of the Con Ed testimony was the same as it had been before the FPC, the difference being that before the Pomeroy Committee it was challenged

* This report was submitted to—and filed without comment by—Governor Rockefeller.

and refuted at virtually every turn. As zoning and planning board officials, local mayors, and school authorities from many communities appeared to plead that Con Ed be compelled to put its high tension lines underground, Con Edison witnesses returned to contend that this would be prohibitively expensive. The utility said it would have to abandon the Storm King project if it was required to resort to underground transmission. Con Ed declared its overhead lines would cost $14 million to install from Storm King to its Millwood station in Westchester County, whereas underground lines would cost $99 million.

This may be the most outlandish misrepresentation put forth by Con Ed in its entire case for the project. The cost to individuals, communities, and society as a whole is never figured in Con Ed estimates of this kind. Overhead lines require steel towers, set in concrete at intervals, along a 250-foot wide lane which must be obtained by purchase and condemnation proceedings. Property values are inevitably depressed along power line rights of way, aside from loss of land use and ugly scars left along a landscape overhung with aerial "spaghetti."

Underground lines are resisted by power companies as a matter of policy in the face of insistence that, like sewers, they belong out of sight. Instead of a 250-foot lane, one of fifteen to twenty-five feet—certainly no more than the width of a one way street—would be required. It might not even have to be bought outright, and it would be quite possible to run it along roadways, perhaps providing walkways or cycle paths, with a minimum of ruin to the landscape or to real estate values.

Con Ed has not been able to show why a narrow underground conduit, now manufactured by several major corporations explicitly for this purpose, should cost eight to ten times as much as the despised overhead installations.

106

One of the FPC Commissioners, Charles Ross, made note of this point when he dissented from the ruling which granted the Storm King license to Consolidated Edison.

Mr. Ross did not believe Con Ed's estimate of $99 million, which three assenting commissioners declined to question. He pointed out that the utilities' fight against putting lines underground anywhere, any time, "is a deadly serious war." He added that "when a utility doesn't wish to do something, it becomes prohibitively expensive."

The Ross dissent notwithstanding, and with the help of Governor Rockefeller on March 9, 1965, the Federal Power Commission handed Storm King Mountain over to Consolidated Edison.

Between the Pomeroy hearings of 1964 and the date of the FPC decision, many citizens had hoped against the inevitable, but by then Governor Rockefeller's long unofficial support of Con Ed was made public. The Pomeroy Committee's unanimous report urged the Governor to intervene in the public interest to ask the FPC to defer decision on the Con Ed project until "this momentous and irreversible alteration of the Hudson landscape" could be studied further.* The report cited discrepancies, omissions, and misrepresentations in the Con Ed testimony and solemnly reminded the Governor of lost water resources, needless risks of water table pollution from reservoirs, and dangers to life and property.

The Governor's response was directed more to a mounting volume of public and editorial protest than to the Pomeroy report, on which he did not publicly comment.

Rockefeller said the "economic benefits" outweighed the disadvantages of the Storm King construction. He felt the project would bring more low cost power to the New

* *The Croton-Cortland News,* December 17, 1964.

York areas. Moreover, he expressed the fear that if Con Ed were denied approval, it might go elsewhere and build a more expensive plant which would be reflected in a rate increase to consumers.

"On balance, in my judgment," said Rockefeller in a letter to Pomeroy, "the values of the project—with proper safeguards for the esthetic during and after construction and with consideration of the importance of the large number of jobs to be provided during construction of the project—outweigh the objections which have been raised to it."

The Christmas air of 1964 was blue with curses and cries of protest. "Power-Plant Arrogance," said the *New York Herald-Tribune*. The *Times* called it "Mr. Rockefeller's Wrong Move," and added:

"His position represents a shocking departure from all that the Governor's family has stood for over the years. . . . The Governor sought to justify his decision by arguing that New York City's economy needs the low-cost power the project would provide. Apparently, he was unaware of the testimony. . . ."

The *Croton-Cortland News,* a small newspaper in the heart of the country to be defaced by overhead power lines, howled: "Governor Rockefeller Goes Wrong" and followed with:

". . . the man who once seemed to have the magic touch to do everything right, has lost it, and now seems to be doing everything wrong. . . . He did not have to make it so plain that he had listened to Con Ed and had not listened to the voice of the people who have raised such an outcry for so long that even the Governor must recognize that this is not a crank protest.

"And surely the Governor . . . could have given better reasons than the ones he gave . . . The testimony . . . was

108

that any period of unusual employment would not extend beyond the construction period."

Repeated appeals were made to the Federal Power Commission, and hearings were opened on several minor matters, but the basic case was unchanged. Throughout all of the furor, many private individuals and organizations sought quietly to reach the Governor to persuade him to review his position and, failing that, sought out his brother Laurance.

Laurance is the Rockefeller brother who is a specialist in parks and conservation. He is Chairman of the New York State Council on Parks, a position to which he was appointed by the Governor. Laurance also heads, controls, or influences most of the major conservation organizations in the United States and, through the Rockefeller Foundation and related enterprises, is the largest single contributor to conservation and parks development in the country. He is a man of enormous influence, which he used to help brother Nelson and Con Ed in the power plant battle.

William H. Osborn, president of the Hudson River Conservation Society, the oldest of its kind in the Hudson Valley, sought to persuade Laurance to do what Pomeroy wanted the Governor to do: ask the FPC to delay for one year a decision on the Storm King project in order to study Con Ed testimony which he felt was both false and incomplete.

On May 27, 1965, Laurance Rockefeller told Osborn in a letter that the suggestion to request a delay "wouldn't get very far and for that reason I don't think we should try it. If the Con Edison project is stopped it will be stopped by the courts and not by the FPC changing its mind. . . . I don't see any point in going through a useless gesture."

As the strongest single voice in the United States—a

109

voice which spoke in resounding terms of cash grants and resources unduplicated by any other—Laurance was in a position to speak out against the Con Ed project and the archaic power of the FPC, whether it was a "useless gesture" or not. From past experience he was aware that a position can be taken because it is just and necessary, because it is part of a militant fight, and that doubt of complete victory does not excuse failure to take a stand.

President Johnson had named Laurance to the White House Conference on Natural Beauty, a project in which Mrs. Johnson was, and remains, interested. At that conference, said Laurance, "there were innumerable suggestions that the FPC, whose power of condemnation transcends the legal ability of any state to keep them from doing what they think they ought to do, should be curbed. But even if this were done it would not be retroactive."

Even before the Pomeroy hearings, Chauncey Stillman, member of an old New York family and donor of important park lands to the state, made overtures both to Laurance Rockefeller and Secretary of the Interior Stewart Udall about the Con Ed project. Stillman found it unbelievable that the Rockefellers would not try to stop, or at least to delay, the hydroelectric installations at Storm King. The Stillman family could address the Rockefellers on terms of common interest in the protection of the Hudson Palisades, the preservation of Black Rock Forest near Storm King Mountain and other landmarks saved from ruination.

Stillman reminded Laurance of their mutual respect for "the Tetons and the Yosemite" and warmly complimented Laurance: "You who have done so much to save places of natural beauty must seriously deplore the plans of Consolidated Edison to cut into the face of Storm King Mountain. It seems close to sacrilege to me, who had

110

thought that the Break Neck-Storm King pass of the Hudson had been made inviolable. This true fjord . . ."

Laurance said he was "happy to have your thinking on this in the light of your experience and the interest of your family in the area." With this cliché out of the way, he said he thought there had been "considerable misunderstanding."

"The proposed power plant is not being built on park lands," he told the man who knew exactly what land the Con Ed project was being built on, "and therefore we have no direct authority in the case." As he told William Osborn, neither he nor the Governor nor the whole State of New York would have any legal authority to stop the FPC even if Con Ed was going to build on park lands.

"Ideally," said Laurance, "we would have liked no project at all, but given the hard fact of the proposal we felt it would be better to *work with the company* to ameliorate the effect of the project on the landscape than to oppose it outright with no assurance of success." There it was again: We can't succeed, why fight it?

"We have persuaded Consolidated Edison to modify the design of the plant to conform with the landscape, to bury its power lines under the river rather than using an overhead crossing. . . . While you may not agree with our judgment or tactics . . . please be assured that we do share your concern. . . ."

Stillman tried again. "If you do share my concern for the long range values involved," he wrote in response to Laurance, "you must be aware that every assistance granted to Con Edison in building this plant is merely one more step towards the industrialization of the Hudson River Gorge and Highlands."

But the discourse was over.

Secretary of the Interior Stewart Udall, in New York

City to speak at a Columbia Club luncheon, suggested that perhaps the Hudson River could be salvaged from Consolidated Edison and the Rockefellers. His language was gentle enough but his position was clear. In due course, President Johnson himself made a mild statement favoring preservation and rehabilitation of the Hudson. Udall's fervor cooled after a time, it was reported, for two reasons: First, funds and cooperation from Rockefeller sources were enormously important in many conservation projects favored by the Department of the Interior; second, federal authorities find it difficult to help prevent a conservation disaster where a state governor favors it.

The Scenic Hudson Preservation Conference appealed the FPC licensing decision in the courts without a shred of assistance from any state or federal government agency. Local governments whose municipalities face tax losses, esthetic damage, and the wreckage of their long range planning concepts, joined with Scenic Hudson in planning the legal brief. The legal firm of Paul, Weiss, Rifkind, Wharton & Garrison presented Scenic Hudson's case in the Federal Court in Foley Square, New York City, late in 1965.

Most ordinary citizens and virtually all of the members of the press seem to have given up trying to determine how and why Nelson Rockefeller supported such an indefensible position. The explanation seems inherent in the family's economic ties to corporate wealth (including Con Edison) and in the personal makeup of Nelson Rockefeller. Consolidated Edison has done nothing more than develop and utilize every element of influence and every public relations trick—some of them scarcely legitimate—to achieve its objective. A corporation, whatever else it is, is fundamentally an instrument to make money. Men of authority in elected public offices can deflect the pursuit

112

of corporate power in the public interest—or try to—if they are so disposed. Governor Rockefeller had chosen not to be disposed.

Rockefeller knew he had painted himself into a corner from which he could probably not emerge with pride. He was not comfortable in the knowledge that Con Ed would have to take over part of the irreplaceable acreage donated by the Stillman family to Black Rock Forest, on top of Storm King, which Harvard University operates to advance the science of silviculture. He knew further that Con Ed, irrespective of the power of the FPC, might not have come this far without his personal intervention in the utility's behalf.

When he was questioned before the New York State Women's Joint Legislative Forum in Albany about the Storm King project, he showed a kind of condescending pique. "I worry a little, ladies," he said, "about the fact that so many people only get excited about something after something has happened." Then the man whose family had bought and preserved the Palisades Park system, Jackson Hole in Wyoming, parts of the Great Smokies, and a piece of the Virgin Islands, suggested there was one thing the people could do if they wanted to preserve the scenic Hudson highlands: raise the money and buy them.

Preposterous as the idea was, it still wouldn't work, for, as Laurance had told Messrs. Osborn and Stillman, the FPC can take lands owned by anybody, even the park land donated and willed to the state itself, and give it to Con Ed. But perhaps the Governor, whose outbreaks of humor are as rare as they are applicable, was jesting. If so, his audience got only his point, not the joke.

The *Patent Trader,* published in Mt. Kisco, New York, is an independent Republican newspaper with high professional and critical standards. Each Christmas time the

113

newspaper runs a tongue-in-cheek feature based on the format of the *New York Times'* "100 Neediest Cases." (It bears no disrespect whatsoever to that newspaper's worthy effort to relieve the indescribable distress of some of New York City's most impoverished families.) The *Patent Trader* feels that it is sometimes the overprivileged who have unfulfilled needs. "When the heart is full and the judgment clouded," it asserts, "we appeal to the Hundred Neediest Cases of Suburbia, a unique charity devoted to relieving misery among the affluent, an offer of understanding to the well-heeled and well-fed. Surely the pangs of surfeit can be as hard to bear as the pangs of want, and desperation multipled by five figures is desperation indeed. Can you withhold the hand of compassion from these unfortunates simply because their checks don't bounce? [We] try to alleviate the mink-lined misery of Upper Westchester. Consider the following cases as your conscience guides you."

Without mentioning the full name of Charles Eble, president of the Consolidated Edison Company, the *Patent Trader* led off in 1964 with:

CASE 1

A Heart in the Highlands

The frustrations of life as an electric utility company president have driven Charles E., 60, to the brink of despair. Some years ago, Mr. E. proposed building a generating station using atomic energy in the middle of Queens, but his hopes were dashed by the hostility of surrounding property holders. Rallying bravely from defeat, this courageous executive set his heart on a reversible pumped storage hydroelectric installation in the Hudson Highlands. Under the sympathetic guidance of the Federal Power Commission he developed plans to knock the top off a mountain and build a reservoir which would supply water to a naturalistic-looking power plant on the river bank. To the dismay of Mr. E., these plans for the improvement of the stark outlines of the Hudson Valley met with bitter resistance from conservationists and property owners along the route of his proposed power line. Only the continuing support of the FPC and an assortment of local politicians has kept him from losing heart entirely.

At present, Mr. E. is managing on a five per cent rate increase which took effect last July, but this provides additional gross annual revenue of only $27 million. Funds are asked to continue the sympathetic support of FPC, which means so much to Mr. E., and to purchase a few more town supervisors to help make this brave man's dream come true.

All of the people who had contributed money and volunteer labor to the Scenic Hudson Preservation Conference, the thousands who had endured rebuffs at the hands of the Federal Power Commission, or who had stood by in silent frustration while Governor Rockefeller steadfastly supported Con Ed's assault on the Hudson Highlands and the great river; all who had recoiled against the faint heart of Laurance Rockefeller and his distaste for a fight unless the outcome could be predetermined, all of these and perhaps millions of other Americans whose voices remained unheard in the three-year conflict that seemed preordained to go against them, received a holiday season surprise a few days after Christmas in 1965.

On December 29 the United States Court of Appeals in a unanimous decision set aside the Federal Power Commission order to license the Con Ed plant at Cornwall.

"The lobby that never fails" had faltered. The FPC, which disclaimed jurisdiction if not interest in conservation, natural beauty, the death of fish life, and the concern of citizens for the ruination of their towns by utility line installations, was coldly rebuked by the court for acting like "an umpire calling balls and strikes" and failing to concern itself with the public interest. It had, in short, acted very much like one monopoly serving another, rather than an agency with a responsibility for larger issues. Commissioner Charles Ross, the lone dissenter, who had cared about the Hudson River, who questioned Con Ed's testimony, was right and the others were wrong: so said the judgment.

The historic decision accomplished a great deal more than setting aside the FPC order; it inferentially rapped the knuckles of all regulatory governmental bodies for failure to give "active and affirmative protection" to the public. This would deny such agencies the pleasure of serving, as they often do, as spokesmen for the operations they are obliged to regulate.

The decision, written by Judge Paul R. Hays and concurred in by Chief Judge J. Edward Lumbard and Judge Sterry R. Waterman, reflected a concern for human life above and beyond the immediate demands of a private corporation, even if supported in its quest by a friendly Governor and a family of immeasurable power. The cost of a project, said Judge Hays, should be "only one" of many factors in the decision to license a monstrous power plant at Storm King Mountain. He reminded the Federal Power Commission, in effect, to become interested in some of the issues and questions it had discarded as beneath or beyond its area of concern.

Said the court: "The record as it comes to us fails markedly to make out a case for the Storm King project on, among other matters, costs, public convenience and necessity, and the absence of reasonable alternatives.

"It is our view, and we find, that the Commission has failed to compile a record which is sufficient to support its decision."

The judges noted that Storm King Mountain, the high-

116

lands, and the Hudson River gorge constitute an area of great beauty and historic significance. The "contention that the Commission must take these factors into consideration in evaluating the Storm King project is justified. . . ."

What the court said and what the people had said in their protest was the same thing.

Consolidated Edison did its best to sound obliging, for a day or so. Having declared it was impossible, owing to excessive cost, to put its transmission lines underground, it now discovered it could put the whole power plant underground at Storm King, out of sight entirely. The utility appealed the court decision and went on a costly binge of buying advertising in metropolitan and Hudson Valley newspapers, pleading for public support and threatening to pollute New York City air with new coal-burning plants if denied the use of Storm King Mountain.

Con Ed was caught in an embarrassing situation, which was expressed by stepped up pugnacity and further public relations activity. No attempt was made to comply with the court's direction to seek an alternative site, such as the abandoned Brooklyn Navy Yard, already an industrial site, or new gas turbine plants, which offer relief from air pollution.

Leo O. Rothschild, Scenic Hudson Conference Chairman, publicly accused Con Ed of continuing to waste stockholders' money on the Storm King project. Undeterred even when Governor Rockefeller later grudgingly reversed his own position on the matter, Con Ed made additional investments in trying to take over the mountain. Mr. Rothschild charged the utility management with spending millions of dollars, which the company "will not be able to recover . . . unless it gets its license . . . to build the plant." The management could plead that with the Governor on its

117

side the decision to spend all that preliminary money appeared to be without risk. But it was an argument that would not please all Con Ed stockholders.

It could not be truly said that the FPC had been beaten in the Con Ed case for the reason that the federal agency was not directly a participant in the court action. The FPC played the role of a biased judge, cheering for Consolidated Edison while its own record and conduct was subjected to critical review. Con Ed and the FPC, contrary to the function of the federal agency, had made common cause against the public interest, yet there remains no certainty that the FPC will not grant another license for the same hydroelectric project.

The FPC simply stood enjoined, following the Federal Court decision, to reopen the hearings and develop a record showing that it took into consideration all the important factors of the Con Ed application that had previously been slighted or ignored. Under the law, the federal agency was empowered, if it so desired, to willfully override the public interest and grant the license anyway, so long as it complied with the court's directions to "complete" its record to show that it had studied alternative power sources, the conservation issue, scenic damage, and so on.

Before the project at Storm King is safely and forever abandoned, the FPC would have to swallow a great deal of pride.

So might Governor Rockefeller. In 1966, he indicated that he rather wished Consolidated Edison would quiet down and try building a power plant somewhere else. He did not indicate whether his changed outlook on the Storm King matter evolved from new knowledge that his previous position was dead wrong, or whether his campaign for reelection had temporarily improved his response to the public interest.

118

6

Pocantico:

DODGING TAXES ON THE EMINENT DOMAIN

The Rockefellers have been around the North American continent a long, long time. The name was German in the seventeenth century and was spelled Rockenfeller, but it showed up minus the "n" with the arrival of a Rhineland immigrant, Johann Peter Rockefeller in the area of Somerville, New Jersey, in 1723. The family may originally have been French Huguenots, who spelled their name Roquefueille and who fled from religious persecution in Southern France. Genealogists in need of exercise might try to establish a relationship between the Rockefellers and the French Huguenot family named Requa (which could be an Americanized corruption) who settled in the Hudson Valley between Peekskill and Mount Pleasant. The name Requa appears on street signs and on tombstones in the Westchester area.

The maternal grandmother of John D. Rockefeller, Sr., was Lucy Avery, a descendant of Christopher Avery, who had come to the colonies with the Puritans in 1630, and who traced his ancestry to English kings. The mother of John D. Rockefeller, Sr., was Eliza Davison, a Scot. The results of this merger of the Scottish-Puritanical characteristics of frugality and religious discipline seem to have been dominant from generation to generation among the Rockefellers. Although there were roisterers and tipplers who

119

bore the Rockefeller name in the nineteenth century, discipline and austerity were the notable family traits.

Nelson Rockefeller's grandfather, John D., Senior, was born in Richford, near Binghamton, New York, on July 8, 1839. When John D. was ten years old, his father, William A. Rockefeller, a well-to-do lumberman and occasional patent medicine salesman, was indicted on a charge of having sexual intercourse with a fifteen-year-old hired girl in his home. The indictment never came to trial, possibly because William fled to the next county—or perhaps because the girl, Anne Vanderbeak, was persuaded that she did not have much of a case. The indictment was announced a year and three months after the alleged rape occurred, indicating that some considerations other than quick justice were involved. It was thought that business associates of William, who had been caught in a horse-stealing scandal, helped press the charge as a means of settling old scores.

William Rockefeller went back to selling medicine and was away from home a great deal. He made money, and there is no evidence to suggest that his son, John D., was ever anything but well off. Thus those later stories, so dearly loved by American mythmakers, suggesting that John D. Rockefeller had risen from an impoverished childhood, are pure fakery. He grew up, happily enough, in the Finger Lakes area, where he learned to love the forests and the landscape with a fervor that is reflected in every square yard of the land at Pocantico Hills.

For high school, John D. and his brother William were sent to Cleveland as boarding students. Within two years, John, a dropout, had signed up for a three-month bookkeeping and commercial law course. He emerged to begin almost at once to work at responsible jobs. From the beginning he showed, first, a flair and, at length, an astounding

120

genius for making money. The fortune he founded has continued to expand on an incremental scale until it is now so vast that its full dimensions could not be fully known without invoking the research resources of many countries.

William Rockefeller was the first of the two boys to leave Cleveland. A young multimillionaire, he had a Manhattan house at 689 Fifth Avenue, and was president of Standard Oil of New York until 1911. He was a trustee of Consolidated Gas Company, a forerunner to Consolidated Edison, and was one of the first ten private customers (as was his brother John) of the New York Steam Company.

It was William who led the Rockefellers to the Sleepy Hollow country of Westchester County. In the 1880s he bought a monumental stone castle, which had been built about 1830, from Edward Bartlett, a New York merchant, and gave it the name of Rockwood Hall. The great Gothic mansion stood on a bluff overlooking the Hudson. After Wiliam died in 1922, Rockwood Hall became a country club and golf course which did not survive the depression, and the Rockefeller family had the mansion torn down. They still own the four hundred odd acres of open river front land that contains some of the most magnificent copper beech trees in the country.

John D. Rockefeller began buying land near, but not contiguous to, William's holdings in the 1890s. He assembled seventeen tracts in and around the village of Pocantico Hills, a roadside community along County House Road, which connected then and now with Bedford Road. Because the former led to the Westchester County Home for the Poor, it was for some years a local joke that the Rockefellers "live on the road to the poorhouse." The seventeen tracts included 150 acres called The Park, in which all the family's various homes were built until Nel-

121

son's two brothers, John-the-Third and David moved into houses outside the walled and fenced enclosure. The original tracts cost John D. Senior $168,705.

The then fifty-five-year-old Oil King began putting together the most valuable residential property on earth today. John D. and his wife Laura (Spelman) Rockefeller, one of the first girls he had met in Cleveland when he was sixteen years old, lived in an old frame mansion, one that had come with the lands. It was destroyed by fire in 1902 and over the next several years a fifty-room stone mansion was built from granite quarried on the property. Of modified Georgian style, it was called Kijkuit, a Dutch word meaning "lookout"—a name justified by the fact that the house commanded an imposing view of the Saw Mill Valley and afforded an unobstructed line of vision thirty miles southward to mid-Manhattan.

Construction of the Rockefeller mansion occurred at a time when many of the great and ornate houses, so much loved by the first and second generation heirs of the Robber Baron age, were built. The Rockefeller house itself was not comparable in cost or design to such examples as Biltmore, built in the 1890s in Asheville, North Carolina, by George W. Vanderbilt. That copy of a French chateau, surrounded by 146,000 acres of land that extended for forty miles in one direction, had 250 rooms, with a dining hall seventy-five feet high. The place still stands as a museum, although the acreage has been reduced to 12,000.*

But the Rockefeller house was splendid enough and a classic of the pre-World War I era. Hundreds of trees, many of them gigantic, were transplanted to the barren

* For a study of this and other costly and venerable properties, see *Great American Mansions and Their Stories,* by Merrill Folsom, Hastings House, New York, 1963. Mr. Folsom is Westchester Bureau chief for the *New York Times* in White Plains, New York.

hill. Some were hauled overland, their roots secure in enormous balls of earth, on special low-wheeled flatbed trailers. At the hilltop site, winches raised them upright and swung them into the previously prepared open earth. Guy wires and lines held them until they took root.

Orange trees were imported from the estate of the Marquis d'Aux at Le Mans in France; very old boxwoods were brought from The Netherlands, larch from Scotland, and yew from England. Jasmine trees, bays, quinces, and gingkos were set into the acreage along with thousands and thousands of rhododendrons, dogwoods, and other plantings.

The estate contained at one time the largest nurseries in the world to provide the land with an ever-growing, ever-blooming supply of flowers and greenery. Between three hundred and five hundred workmen, in addition to household and service help, worked on the site in the course of construction and preparation of the grounds. Artisans were brought to Pocantico from Europe and the Orient; native specialists and people of particular skills were employed as required. Bulwarks and balustrades, terraces and portals, brooks, trails and stately rose gardens ornamented the hilltop site. There were hidden nooks and leafy bowers to provide quiet settings from which to look out upon the vista of the shimmering Hudson. The view from Kijkuit was, as John D. Rockefeller III said some years ago, "almost too panoramic." The latter rebelled against all of the care, cropping and formal garden style of outdoors when he built his own home on the estate, and took to a more informal kind of country life.

A tunnel was built into a subbasement, disappearing through a kind of ledge in a man-made rock cliff, so that trucks could remove trash and ashes without ever coming into view from the walks or gardens.

Tom Pyle, who worked on the estate as a grounds man, security guard, and warden over a fifty-year period, watched the house and lands take shape, and described the process with a kind of breathless wonder in a book published in 1964.* Mr. Pyle tells of the building of tiers of gardens from which fountains spilled their overflow into a Japanese brook which winds and circles down from the house, across the main drive and into a serene pond graced with a small pebbled island accessible by steppingstones. The brook continues now through Laurance Rockefeller's estate until it is swallowed up in a storm drain and carried off downhill into the Sleepy Hollow country.

Pyle worked on the brook with crews of artisans for two summers but does not remember exactly how long it took to finish building. Inlaid cobblestones form the bottom of the stream, which varies in width from fifteen inches to two feet. As it swirls from pool to pool, it creates little waterfalls beside a graveled path that crosses and recrosses the moving work of art over arched wooden bridges. It passes, at one point, a small Japanese temple. The edges of the brook are rolled banks of grass which must be continually shorn with hand clippers along its entire length of perhaps five hundred yards. The brook and its plantings require the care and skill of year-round workmen.

Tom Pyle remembered John D. Senior making one of the most dryly innocent and unintentionally comic remarks ever attributed to him. Mr. Rockefeller was leading a guest along the full length tour of the Oriental garden stream and, addressing himself to the visitor, was overheard to say:

"You know, these little brooks run mighty high!"

Monuments and statuary and archways, cropped plant-

* *Pocantico, Fifty Years on the Rockefeller Domain,* by Tom Pyle as told to Beth Day; Duell, Sloan & Pearce, New York, N.Y., 1964.

ings, acres of free-form and geometrically designed flower beds dotted the meticulously cared for landscape at the home of the controlled and thoughtful little man who refined in his lifetime the two great skills of achieving wealth and disposing of it constructively.

In assembling, building, creating, and extending the estate at Pocantico Hills; in shaping the earth itself, making it fruitful; in transporting ancient trees to stand as if indigenous to their alien site, in cutting granite from the hills and chiseling it into forms to shape the hilltop house, Mr. Rockefeller "showed people what God could have done if He'd had any money." * Other great and lavish mansions were built in that period, but none has grown to such enormous value for the reason that none has remained the household of a family which continued through the years to add land holdings while pressed on all sides by the demands of metropolitan development.

The interior of the mansion admitted a great deal of natural light and was not as dark and somber as many large residences of the period. The style was later brightened and made more cheerful through enlightened interior design treatment. Nevertheless, the old house has period piece characteristics that Nelson, in particular, is uninhibitedly fond of—notwithstanding his preference for modern art that, while conventionally acceptable today, was avant garde when he was one of its moneyed proponents. People who years ago were visitors or guests in the place speak of having come upon dark and burnished bronzes, "the sort of thing you might idly study while waiting for the elevator at Brooks Brothers."

One man, who has served the Governor in a profes-

* This line is from an old vaudeville monologue and crops up now and then in biographical accounts, usually attributed to a contemporary personality reputed to be witty.

sional capacity, tells of a recent visit to one of the baths, built circa 1911, with its oversized marble shower.

"It is truly a splendid place," he said, "with large brass and silver wheels which you turn to bring on and turn off various sprays, to control the force of the water and of course the temperature of it. It is secure and solid and it looks and feels rather like one of those well-appointed movie submarines of pre-World War II days that had somehow got stood on end. There was one large wheel, about midsection, that I particularly liked to turn on, just for the hell of it, because I had never seen its function duplicated anywhere else. It gives you a strong, almost unbearable jet where you might expect, and the disk that fills the center of the silver wheel is marked, 'Kidney Spray.' I made some comment to Governor Rockefeller at breakfast about the house in general, and about the shower with its kidney spray. He smiled and welcomed the comment and said he was just crazy about the old place and wouldn't change anything in the shower for the world."

Two old communities, the hamlet of Eastview and the commuter town of Pocantico Hills, were obliterated in the acquisition of land and in the building of the Rockefeller estate. Pocantico Hills, also known as Tarrytown Heights, was on the verge of lively commercial development about the time John D. Rockefeller retired from a full-time business life and began buying parcels of land in the area. Doctors had told him to slow down the pace of his work, which he did with a kind of concentration and devotion that enabled him to outlive his advisors. He lived for nearly half a century after thinking over his doctors' counsel. He put agents to work acquiring land close to the Hudson Valley region where his brother William lived in splendor. Failure of a local real estate development undoubtedly worked in John D.'s favor; Mr. Rockefeller was almost always lucky that way, luck being a factor in the affairs and fortunes of men.

In the early 1890s, plans were afoot to subdivide 280 lots on land that had been a part of the former Mallory estate on the hills above Tarrytown. It had long been estate country; in fact, the land along the valley had been for the most part in the hands of the wealthy and had been beautifully preserved from the time of the Dutch manorial holdings of the seventeenth century.

Lewis Roberts, one of the men who financed the building of the Northern Railroad in 1880, is supposed to have seen to it that the line ran through his real estate holdings in the Pocantico Hills area. The Northern was the name for the "Old Putt," or Putnam, Division of the New York Central Railroad and it ran from Manhattan to Brewster, New York, cutting along the Saw Mill River to Van Cortlandt, past Yonkers and northward to Elmsford, Tarrytown Heights, Eastview, Briarcliff, and on to Millwood, Yorktown, Somers, and Brewster.

A great public auction was planned and widely advertised to lure land buyers to Pocantico Hills, described as the most elevated point—450 feet above sea level—along the lower Hudson and noted for its clean, bracing mountain air. It was said to be the "healthiest" of all New York's suburbs, although there could have been little difference between one elevated Hudson Valley point and another as far as human health was concerned.

The 280 lots to be sold at public auction on October 22, 1891, by Wilson Blackwell & Co. of New York City, were described in mouth-watering prose in a brochure, with map and text, passed out freely in downtown New York.*

---

* An account of the planned auction appeared in *The Tarrytown Daily News,* on January 12, 1966, under the name of Wally Buxton, pen name of William Gross, who had come into possession of an 1891 brochure promoting the Pocantico Hills development. Mr. Gross is a writer of local lore.

The healthy hilltop site was eighty minutes from the Rector Street station in lower Manhattan by connecting express trains to Pocantico over the Sixth and Ninth Avenue Elevated Railroads. In those days, a commuter to a Wall Street office could board an elevated train to 155th Street and Eighth Avenue in upper Manhattan and change to the Old Putt for the trip to Westchester. The cost to Pocantico Hills from any one of the forty stations on the Sixth or Ninth Avenue Elevated lines in Manhattan was thirteen-and-a-half cents per trip.

The auctioned acreage was glowingly described as abounding in orchards and woodlands, with lots available in five dollar monthly installments after a down payment of 10 per cent, plus the auctioneer's fee.

Moreover, the land was restricted, or zoned, to forbid offensive use of it. No bone-boiling establishments, slaughterhouses, soap factories, or cattle yards were allowed. Livery stables and establishments for the sale of "spirituous or malt liquors" were outlawed. On certain streets, it was stipulated, no building could be erected that cost less than $2,500. On others, the limit was only $1,500.

The auction itself, which was to launch Pocantico Hills into the big time as a commuter town, was part of a project involving the Title Guarantee and Trust Company, with its capital and surplus of $2,400,000, which would guarantee all titles and receive monthly installment payments. Money to build the homes could be borrowed. A substantial free lunch was promised at the auction, along with a concert by the Tarrytown Band at intermission during the sale.

But something kept happening to require postponement of the great sale. The customers never swung off the trains at the little Tarrytown station to see the property with its one thousand feet of frontage along Bedford Road. Time

128

after time, the gala affair to sell off the lots was planned—
and then postponed. As a commuter town, Pocantico Hills
never really hit the big time. In fact, it died away altogether.

It was absorbed into the Rockefeller estate as its hotels,
shops, general store, gas stations, its roundhouse turntable
which swung the Old Putt steam engines around, its post
office and other accoutrements of town life were bought
and demolished or moved elsewhere. A number of dwellings inside The Park, which became in time the enclosed
section of the estate, were moved to the roadside along
the now familiar Route 117 (Bedford Road). All the
dwellings are rental properties owned by the Rockefellers;
most are painted white and all look serene, comfortable and
composed, like the elements of a quietly elegant company
town. There remain in the area once embraced by Pocantico Hills only a few individually owned properties that
have not come into Rockefeller hands.

The small nearby hotels were actually summer resorts
patronized in season and on weekends by people from New
York City who disembarked from the chugging steam trains
of the Old Putt. Small but handsome stations, designed in
the English countryside style fondly cherished by devotees
of rail travel, were torn down both at Pocantico Hills and
at Eastview. The latter was a hamlet of some twenty houses,
a store, a post office and a freight and passenger depot
which served the county poorhouse and Grasslands Hospital.

Before the railroad stations were demolished, however,
it was necessary to remove the railroad itself. The coal-
burning steam engines rattled their way through the south-
east section of the estate, confined to their own right of
way by trackside fencing. The fences could keep the
nomadic hoboes, hunters, and trackwalkers from trespassing onto the estate grounds, but could not hold back the

129

billowing steam and sooty smoke that the engines expelled. By this time, John D. Rockefeller, Sr., was perhaps the country's best known golfer, recognized as a friendly caricature in knickers and cap—with a pocketful of nickels, later upgraded to dimes, for distribution and image-building.

Part of the golf course paralleled the railroad tracks and the smoke and steam constituted an intolerable nuisance to Mr. Rockefeller and his cleanly groomed guests. John D., Jr., took on the job of negotiating a track relocation operation which made life infinitely more endurable on the golf course. The relocation eliminated, at a cost to the Rockefellers of $700,000, not only a section of railroad, but two entire communities. The site of the old Pocantico depot was turned back into open landscape and the roadbed of the old tracks became carriage trails.

Next to be relocated was St. Joseph's College, operated by the Christian Brothers Catholic order. It was moved from its farmland setting between Pocantico Hills and the village of Pleasantville to Barrytown, New York.

As Tom Pyle told Beth Day, a staff writer for *Reader's Digest* who did Pyle's book, the relocation of St. Joseph's College and its cemetery gave him a welcome opportunity to engage in a ghoulish form of moonlighting. The chief administrator of the school, Brother Julian, had not been eager to move the religious institution to Barrytown, but he was no less able to resist the realities of materialism than the New York Central Railroad. When Nelson's father, John D., Jr., raised his offer for the place to an irresistible $1,500,000 cash—plus free relocation of the cemetery as a fringe benefit—it was Moving Day for St. Joseph's and the Christian Brothers, both the quick and the dead.

The quick got away first and Tom Pyle was employed by Brother Julian to keep an eye on the personal effects of the departing brothers while the seminarians carefully removed the grave markers from the little cemetery plot. A small steam shovel was brought in and it began dipping its bucket into the graveyard, scooping up caskets and gingerly dropping them into open trucks for the road trip to Barrytown, where the remains and the grave markers were coordinated, and where the reinterred now rest in eternal peace, presumably unaware of their change of address.

Old John D., Sr., had other troubles with his golf course before things settled down to the measured control required at Kijkuit. Flocks of sheep which grazed on the fairways provided both a grass-cutting function and served as living props for a pastoral setting. Groundskeepers were always at hand to prepare the greens and the fairways, removing early morning dew from the greens when necessary and brushing away snow if Mr. Rockefeller planned to play on unseasonable days. For years, he was such a golf fanatic that he would often play under the most adverse weather conditions.

The inevitable failure of groundskeepers to locate and remove from the cropped fairways every solitary obstruction deposited by the serenely grazing sheep unfortunately stopped an occasional rolling golf ball short, thus making subsequent approach shots uncertain if not untidy. Distractions caused by the inability to reconcile the bucolic with a clean fairway shot resulted in the banishment of the flocks to more distant pastures.

Another Catholic order, the Sisters of Mercy, operated an orphanage for girls at a site beyond one of the entrance gates. The nuns and their young charges were welcome on the estate grounds at times as long as no fuss or bother ensued. Girls from still another Catholic institution, Marymount College, also strolled the grounds, which merged with the school's own campus. Following an unpleasant incident in which some visitors, out walking with the Sisters of Mercy girls, affronted old Mr. Rockefeller, word went out from Kijkuit that The Park was thereafter closed to the Sisters and their visitors. Someone had yelled "Hey, Johnny!" at old John D. as his chauffeur, Vincent, drove him past the group, and Mr. Rockefeller was quite upset over it.

Today the Sisters of Mercy are well situated with their school on a riverfront site in Dobbs Ferry, about eight miles south of Kijkuit. Their properties and land were bought by the Rockefellers for a sum reported to be half a million dollars, and the site of the old place, on which the buildings were leveled, is now open fields.

Marymount College, alone of the old institutions near the estate, remains and flourishes on the hill next to Kijkuit, and the school has at times acknowledged receipt of generous assistance from the neighboring family.

The original park was closed off, and elaborate security measures became common practice after the visitation of a group of pickets. One of the Rockefeller corporations, the Colorado Fuel and Iron Company, was involved in serious labor difficulties that led to massacre and tragedy in Ludlow, Colorado. John D. Rockefeller, Jr., owned 40 per cent of the mining company, but was not directly involved in the management of the operations in the west, nor had he attended director's meetings. Nevertheless, when company police and hired thugs shot up the mining camp—a tent community where striking employees lived— national outrage was understandably directed at the Rockefellers. Federal troops finally restored order to the camp, but militant "Wobblies," members of the Industrial Workers of the World, picketed the Pocantico Hills estate and the

132

Standard Oil Company offices at 26 Broadway in downtown New York.

Stockade fences, impregnable gates, and day and night security guards became the rule at Pocantico. This ended any further casual strolling through the grounds, but most of the acreage outside the enclosure remained accessible within certain limitations. Although more and more of the estate grounds have been fenced off in recent years, much of the network of seventy-five miles of riding trails are today open to riders, and trespassing laws on the posted lands are seldom, if ever, enforced against people who do not abuse the privilege or who do not litter the landscape. Guards direct trespassers with guns or hunting dogs to leave at once, but the power to make arrests, which some guards have if they are licensed wardens, is seldom exercised.

The old days of kidnaping scares and electrified fences no longer prevail on the Rockefeller lands, which are surrounded now by a ring of towns and villages with radio-equipped police cars. Nearby are headquarters of the New York State Police, the New York Thruway patrol, and the Westchester County parkway police.

After the elder John D. died in 1937, the supreme command of the estate was handed down to John D., Jr., who had long since given up business activities to devote himself exclusively to the management of charitable, research, and educational enterprises established by the family fortune. Actually, Junior had taken over most of the estate management tasks anyway; his father's interest in the place lagged in the late 1920s, when he began to spend more time at his homes in Ormond Beach, Florida, and Lakewood, New Jersey.

John D., Jr., added considerable acreage to the estate

133

by purchasing contiguous parcels of land from time to time. Also some acreage was given away or transferred— not much of it was ever sold. In fact, the sale of land to Consolidated Edison Company is one of the rare instances of any Rockefeller land transaction involving the receipt of money. Rockefeller land was given away for schools, fire departments, recreation projects, and a hospital.

The family gave the land for and in fact built Union Church at Pocantico Hills, a small gem of a building with stained glass windows by Marc Chagall and Henri Matisse. The Matisse window was the last work of art undertaken by the French master.

Jules Abels, in his account of *The Rockefeller Billions,* writes that the Rockefeller estate at one time exceeded seven thousand acres, but this appears to be an error in a superbly researched work. It is likely that the figure included Rockefeller lands not actually part of the family estate at Pocantico Hills, which has probably never exceeded 4,500 acres.

The only time the press was allowed to go into the enclosed section of the estate was on October 19, 1959, when the Governor's son Steven was married to Miss Anne Marie Rasmussen, the family's Norwegian maid with whom young Steven had fallen in love. Possibly under the heady influence of romance, reporters estimated the size of the estate as being as low as 2,500 acres and as high as 4,180. A year later, when Tom Pyle was hailed by Anne Marie and Steven to "come see our new baby," which was asleep in the carriage, the venerable old friend of Steven's reflected that he was looking on the fifth generation of Rockefellers he had known on the "vast rolling twenty-five hundred acres of land that comprise" the Pocantico Hills estate. Thus even those who walked the land could be misinformed as to its dimensions.

The Rockefeller estate is largely in the township of Mount Pleasant, but bits and pieces of it extend into three other political subdivisions—North Tarrytown, Tarrytown, and the township of Greenburgh. At the beginning of 1966, it was composed of one tax-free cemetery and 163 parcels of taxable land adding up to 3,667.92 acres. It is nearly ten times the size of the principality of Monaco, where 25,000 people live, and nearly five times larger than New York's Central Park, which is the legal residence of nobody at all. In this area of a little less than six square miles, there are about seventy separate structures, ranging from Kijkuit itself and a million dollar playhouse to tidy, utilitarian storage sheds, stables, and kennels. The estate has its own water reservoirs, a bomb shelter, a private lodge for the Governor, a few small lakes, a coach barn, a couple of historical sites and an infinite number of quiet glades and glens. There are several high spots which allow panoramic views of the Hudson Valley.

There are individual residences for all of the Rockefeller brothers except Winthrop, who lives in Arkansas. One interesting dwelling is a house designed by the architect Marcel Breuer, which was first erected in the garden of the Museum of Modern Art in Manhattan. The house was the showcase feature of a special exhibit; when it was concluded Mr. Breuer's creation was dismantled in carefully prepared sections and trucked to Pocantico Hills, where Winthrop, who was living there briefly, took it over.

Winthrop lived at Pocantico for a time with his first wife, Bobo, from whom he was divorced at a settlement cost of nearly six million dollars, after which he married Mrs. Jeanette Edris and took up, in Arkansas, large scale ranching and farming and, eventually, ran for Governor.

During Nelson's mariage to Mary Todhunter Clark, he lived in the old Hawes House, at which his divorced wife

135

remained in residence until she acquired a home on the far other end of Westchester County. When he isn't in Albany or at his New York residence or in Venezuela, Governor Rockefeller and Happy live at Kijkuit with their second family.

The responsibility for running the estate normally fell, after the death of John D., Jr., to the very reserved and respected John D. the Third, which is just the way the name is spoken when it is necessary to distinguish him from the other Rockefellers. However, John (the identifying appendages are dropped here for the present) had long ago found a spot on the land as far away from the big stone place of his father and grandfather as he could go and still remain on family land. It was and remains a lovely, if modest, place on a rocky hill, just off Old Sleepy Hollow Road and the Albany Post Road, between the towns of Tarrytown and Ossining. John's place is identified by a simple roadside sign bearing the farm's name, Fieldwood, and a painted likeness of a black bull. Aberdeen Angus cattle breeding stock are a principal product of the farm.

John's house and grounds differ from the others not only in remoteness but in the casual, unostentatious environment. John runs what an English countryman would call a proper farm. His land is used for grazing, with his meadows fenced off and pasture allowed time for regrowth after sheep and cattle have taken off the grass. Fieldwood is a professional farm in the full sense, and while the land around John's residence is neat and attractive, there is little of the pool-table lawns with perfect edging and movie set gardens that he had grown to dislike in the enclosed Park.

Although something of a loner, John is warmly liked by his neighbors and he lives in closer relationships with off-estate people than other Rockefeller residents on the

136

Kijkuit property. He has often been seen driving his sedate black Humber over back roads or scooting about in an open jeep, roughly shod, jacketed and sporting a battered hat, looking very much like the lean and serious farmer he is. The raising of fine Black Aberdeen Angus is a very serious business at Fieldwood Farm as the *Drover's Journal,* trade paper of the cattle business, sometimes reports in accounts of the origins and sales of highly prized stock.

John's love for his land is unmistakably apparent, but it appears to be an unsentimental interest for good land *in use* rather than property for retreat and adornment. Anyone who knows the way can drive to John's house unchallenged by guards or walk across pastures and reach the place without being impeded by the chain link fences common to much of the Rockefeller property.

It was John who, after John D., Jr., died, changed the autocratic rules that had always been in effect on the estate—rules which obliged members of the family to make reservations for a horse to ride, even though the animals stood idle in stalls, rules which called for the expulsion of strollers who so much as picked a dandelion. John's own children had to learn to saddle and groom their horses, but the rules were intended to respect the sense of things, rather than enforce discipline for its own sake.

Not long ago, Mr. John, as farm hands and employees call him, mentioned to one of the men who manages some of the farm operations that the presence of an unsightly shack along the boundary line of one of his fields was a pity. The shed was in the rear yard of a man who has a small house on a small lot that extends to the edge of Fieldwood Farm. It is not likely that the man in question ever thought of the possibility of his decrepit outbuilding adding a disturbing element to an otherwise esthetic view. The condition of cluttered back yards and their background effect on a vista across an open meadow evoke no response from people who have not learned, by cultivation or observation, to care for land and property. Mr. Rockefeller's distaste for ugliness and litter is well known, and shared by Fieldwood people who themselves have a feeling for well-tended property.

When one of the men told Mr. Rockefeller that he knew the owner of the property on which the ramshackle shed stood, and that he would be willing to talk with the fellow and help him repair or remove the eyesore, Mr. Rockefeller declined. His affection for an environment free of junk and his concern for keeping the land beautiful wherever possible would not allow him to intrude on the private world of another man.

"He has so little," Mr. Rockefeller reflected, "and I have so much; it would not be kind to mention the matter."

John is concerned about the feelings of others to an extent that he is beloved—there is no other word for it—by some of those around the farm, employees and adjoining landowners alike. The neighbors generally exclude Mr. John by name from the increasingly harsh criticism voiced against "the Rockefellers," by which is meant largely the Governor. It is the latter who is the main target for critical talk; he is the one who is in politics and thus exposed to the main attack.

Fieldwood Farm people are carefully chosen for their jobs, not in terms of a screening process to determine their capacity or special abilities, but to minimize the possibility that any of them might have to be dismissed for any reason at all. It is common knowledge around the farm that Mr. John is distressed when any man has to be given notice for fear that he will be "disappointed in himself." The possibility that people will despair or be disappointed in themselves is prevalent enough in life and Mr. John does not,

138

by the careless selection of employees, care to be the cause
of any more of it.

Local governments obligingly allow the Rockefellers
virtually full possession of several public roads or sections
of them that are enveloped by the estate grounds. Two of
them, Gory Brook Road and Pocantico Lake Road, are not
maintained as thoroughfares at all and are often in non-
passable condition after rainfall or snow. The intent is
to discourage public use of the town roads, to cut down
on littering, trespassing, picknicking, and so on. It doesn't
work, however. Despite the threat of car trouble, some
people use these roads to invade the Rockefeller estate
lands for their own reasons.

An unpaved lane which runs along a famous stream
presents the Rockefellers with daily demonstrations of
man's reprehensible conduct. The public lane is known
as Gory Brook Road. The Rockefellers have tried for many
years to close the road to automobiles and convert it to a
pedestrian or cycling trail, but politics and local law prevented it. As Governor, Nelson has been able to propose,
command, execute, and legislate, but as the dominant property owner in Mount Pleasant, he and the whole family
have aroused ire and faced defeat each time they have
sought to have Gory Brook Road closed or to have Route
117 (Bedford Road) realigned to better serve the estate.

Gory Brook Road cuts directly through the estate on
a north-south line. The Rockefellers own the land on both
sides of the town road and there are no dwellings or structures along its unpaved length. It is lovely woodland, crisscrossed by streams which run under arched stone bridges.
But there is something about Gory Brook Road that brings
out the swinish, littering conduct of humankind. It is a
setting of consummate beauty, a lover's lane, a wild life

sanctuary, and a foul, junk-strewn mess all in one. The combination has taxed the patience of the Rockefellers and offended hikers and strollers for many years.

Workmen have placed neatly painted oil drums, with covers chained to them, at rustic parking sites along the lane and specifically at places where the brook runs beside the road. This is where people go to wash their cars. The trash cans are regularly found hurled into the brook, the lids having been removed and sailed into the woods. On the grounds are discarded soft drink containers and the inevitable beer cans, facial tissues, cigarette stubs, cigar butts, old-fashioned rubber contraceptives, greasy rags, and empty cans of car polish. On occasion even bedsprings and junked kitchen appliances have been found. Gates to nearby riding trails have been lettered with obscenities, indicating that some visitors carry brush and paint in their cars in preparation for any opportunity to extend the circulation of their scatological graffitti.

All of the Rockefellers, and indeed all of the estate employees, from the beginning, were trained and directed to appreciate natural beauty and to pick up litter anywhere and any time it was observed. When David Rockefeller, now president of the Chase Manhattan Bank, and youngest of Nelson's brothers, was a youth, he was visited at Kijkuit by a Philadelphia girl, Peggy McGrath, whom he was courting at the time and whom he later married. David and Peggy were strolling along a trail one day and Peggy, peeling and eating an orange, tossed bits of the peel aside as she walked along. When David saw what she had done he went back along the way they had come, picked up the orange peels, and put them into the pocket of his jacket, then returned to Peggy and said gently:

"We don't litter here."

Residents of the estate area and riders appreciative

of the privilege of cantering over the remarkably beautiful cinder trails on the grounds are infuriated when they observe some outlander toss a beer can or a Kleenex from a car window while motoring over the crowned back roads around the Rockefeller countryside. One day about three years ago, two ladies in jodhpurs, emerging in an open car from Sleepy Hollow Country Club stables after a horseback ride through the estate, saw a two-toned car filled with adults and children. Daddy was driving and Mommy was sitting beside him, and in the back seat were an uncertain number of children, and all were eating. The two ladies were driving behind the family of tourists on the narrow road that runs along the walled fields in which a herd of Black Aberdeen Angus was munching grass. They were suddenly shocked to see father and mother simultaneously extend their arms from the front windows and drop banana peels on the road, while from one of the rear windows a tin can was propelled.

The equestriennes brought their open car to a halt, gathered up the banana skins and the tin can and took after the insensate family. They caught up with the mobile garbage disposal unit at the juncture of Old Sleepy Hollow Road where the car had paused to allow its occupants to observe the scenery they had not yet littered. One of the pursuing ladies got out of the car, walked over to the parked sedan and dropped into the father's lap two banana peels and one damp tin can, and said to all of them in a level voice:

"You dropped these."

The ladies found the experience therapeutic, and they like to think that John D.-the-Third, who wouldn't consider doing such a thing himself, might have been pleased.

The Black Aberdeen Angus herds graze in open fields along the blacktop road that separates the Sleepy Hollow

Country Club from John's working farm, and weekend motorists have caught on to the fact that in an hour's drive from New York they can take their kids to a great farm with real animals. It is a tourist attraction, mercifully on a small scale thus far, but a very beautiful one, for the great beasts standing in black silhouette against the velvet green slope, with the Hudson in the background haze, make a memorable picture for city dwellers.

Since John III was not interested in the titular role he might have been expected to fulfill, the estate went corporate. In October of 1960, the Greenrock Corporation was formed and the president of the new company was Victor Borella, a Dartmouth classmate of Nelson's, who had been associated with the Governor and with Rockefeller interests in one way or another most of his adult life. Borella had been a kind of labor relations adviser to Nelson while, concurrently, presiding over the Rockefeller Center operation.

Stock in the new corporation was held equally by John D., Nelson, Laurance, and David, leaving only Winthrop and their sister, Abby Mauze, out of it because they were otherwise not involved. The general manager of the new family company is Lester Sleinkofer, superintendent of the estate under John D., Jr. Vice president of the operation was Charles T. Keppel of Montrose, New York, who has been on Nelson's personal staff—as distinguished from his staff that may be on a public payroll—since 1948. John P. Hodgkins, formerly of the auditing and accounting empire of Price Waterhouse but now an associate of the Messrs. Rockefeller, was named treasurer, while legal counsel became the responsibility of Robert Orr, of the firm of Milbank, Tweed, Hope and Hadley, the corporation's secretary.

Victor Borella, from the offices he occupied as executive vice president of Rockefeller Center, made a curious announcement to the press when formation of the Greenrock Corporation was disclosed. He said no "drastic changes" were contemplated at the estate, "now or in the future." He did say, however, that "studies have been made and are continuing as to future operations." It was further understood that the Rockefeller land holdings would thereafter be under the jurisdiction not only of the Rockefeller men themselves, but of the Greenrock Corporation and a third power, the Hills Realty Company, which handles the family's real estate transactions. The Hills Realty Company is not in any telephone book, either in the Tarrytown area or in New York City, but like a number of family and state government operations, is located in Rockefeller quarters on the fifty-sixth floor at 30 Rockefeller Plaza in Manhattan.

Hills Realty is the owner of record of about a hundred parcels of Rockefeller land, together with buildings or improvements they contain. Individually, the four Rockefeller brothers held Pocantico estate property in their own names assessed at $3,333,595 in the year 1965 while the Hills Realty Company paid taxes on property assessed at $1,782,200. Total assessed valuation of the estate was the sum of the two figures, or $5,115,795.

Under an equalization formula, a system by which only a portion of the full value of property is taxed in Westchester municipalities, the Rockefeller holdings are assessed at thirty-three per cent. This means that the valuation of $5,115,795 isn't the full value at all, but only the assessment for taxation purposes. The actual value would be three times that amount, or $15,347,385.

Thus, the 3,668 acres of land and all structures, plus improvements over a period of eighty-five years since William Rockefeller began to acquire the property, are now declared by the Town of Mount Pleasant to have a value of a little more than $15.3 million. It is a fantastically modest computation.

In the depth of the American depression in the 1930s, when a hundred families lived on the estate, the value of the land alone was reported at fifty million dollars. The land acreage was substantially less then than it is now— probably about 1,500 acres less. By no exercise of arithmetic or assessment could land valued at fifty million dollars thirty-five years ago be worth less today. Land values, depending on location and protection afforded by zoning laws, have doubled and redoubled several times in the past generation.

A measure of the generosity which taxation computers appear to be extending to the Rockefellers may be detected in a study of the levies against a small bit of residential property in the same unincorporated area of Mount Pleasant that contains the Rockefeller holdings. It is a piece of property that is surrounded on three sides by Rockefeller land and protrudes in a one-acre notch, into a section of estate fields and woodlands. Except for the fact that the small property has not received the loving and costly care lavished upon estate lands, it is little different from Rockefeller acreage. Until recently, six people lived on the property, which had on it a hundred-year-old dwelling that had no value until it could be restored and made suitable for habitation, and a workshop converted into a three-room dwelling for two of the six persons. Total taxes paid on the small property described here are $400 per acre.

If the 3,668 acres of Rockefeller land, including its full complement of residences and other real property, were taxed at the same rate as the one acre it envelops, the total tax bill would have been $1,466,800 in the last year, instead of the $368,000 actually paid. Or putting the comparison

144

another way, if the small property paid taxes at the same rate as the Rockefellers, the total tax levy would have been not $400 but $100.

Admittedly, dollar-for-dollar and acre-for-acre comparisons on such a scale do not tell the complete story of land and property values, but whatever system of computation is in use, favoritism is extraordinarily loaded in the interests of the Rockefellers.

Although the Mount Pleasant Town Board, which governs the town, shows a financial consideration for Rockefeller interests not common to all taxpayers, some benefits are extended to other friendly landowners, among them Consolidated Edison, Union Carbide Company, and International Business Machines (IBM). The Pocantico Hills School District, which is the one that claims Rockefeller estate school taxes, has a tax rate of $42 per $1,000 of assessed valuation. Other Mount Pleasant School districts have rates up to $80 per $1,000.

The school district has, despite its location in the center of a heavy concentration of private and corporate wealth, a poor library, in cramped inadequate quarters; it is open to the public only fourteen hours each week on a yearly budget of $3,300. Plans have been under way for some time, especially in view of the swelling student population of the Mount Pleasant area, to build a modern library with updated services. All school districts were expected to direct a share of their assessed taxes toward the project, since the library is intended to serve the entire unincorporated township. However, protests against assessments to help pay for the library began reaching the Town Board from the Pocantico Hills district. It was unofficially reported that Lester Sleinkofer, general manager of the Greenrock Corporation, was against the project on the grounds that the present school library fulfilled local research and study obligations. Official objections to the library reached the town board from Rockefeller estate employees and occupants of Hills Realty property.

In 1963 a bill slipped through the Legislature and was approved by the school district's most renowned resident (who happened to be Governor at the time), which allowed the Mount Pleasant Board to exclude Pocantico Hills from paying any of the cost of the library. It is the only part of the township thus privileged. The library is being built in Pleasantville at a cost of about half a million dollars, and because of the extraordinary treatment accorded the Pocantico Hills taxpayers, which contains ten million dollars in tax assessments, all the other taxpayers must pay 25 per cent more to meet the cost of the library project. Rockefeller property accounts for approximately half of the lost millions in library assessments, the other half being saved by corporate property in the district owned by the ubiquitous Consolidated Edison, and by Union Carbide, IBM, and the remainder of the people who reside there.

This development naturally caused a good deal of teeth-gritting among that part of the populace of 37,000 who were obliged to make up the difference out of their own pockets if they wanted the town to have a library. The total cost of the library project to be borne by the town taxpayers, excluding the Pocantico Hills well-heeled elite, will amount to $1,650,000 over a thirty-year debt contract period, although this sum probably will be reduced by federal aid.

The library issue was unusual in that it did not remain quiet, as do most issues involving Rockefeller holdings. It became an issue in the campaign for Town Supervisor, the top elected office, in the 1965 elections. Mrs. Henrietta B. Coombs of Pleasantville, without the ghost of a chance of winning, campaigned against her Republican adversary primarily as an exercise in communications. At kaffee-klatsches and wherever she could get an audience, she raised the question of the tax generosity afforded the Rockefeller estate and told the story of the library project. She charged the Town Board with governing "in secret" and called for an updated form of township government. Mrs. Coombs's opponent, who won handily, was horrified at the suggestion that the town government be changed in any way. "What would Pocantico Hills say?" he asked in shocked tones.

Actually, Pocantico Hills is so courteous, quiet, and discreet that only rarely does any direct word or expression of viewpoint sift down from the lofty hilltop barony. When Mrs. Coombs sought to smoke out the Hills Realty Company on the library question, she produced a copy of a letter from the Clerk of the Pocantico Hills School District to the Town Board, protesting payments of library assessments as required of other districts. The School District Clerk had sent letters to all residents, urging them to file similar protests. Copies of these communications, Mrs. Coombs found, were sent to Hills Realty Company, Con Edison, and Union Carbide.

Seven letters of protest against inclusion of Pocantico Hills in the library project finally reached the Town Board as a result of this promotional effort, according to veteran Republic Town Supervisor Earle W. Parsons. Mrs. Coombs said every one of them was from a Rockefeller employee or tenant. She thought the Rockefellers (Hills Realty) had some explaining to do and told them she "found it hard to believe that either of you would knowingly shirk from paying your fair share of this needed town facility."

John E. Lockwood, vice president of Hills Realty, said he had "no information as to why the Clerk of the Pocantico Hills School Board sent to Hills Realty and to others a copy of his letter . . . urging exclusion of the Pocantico Hills School District." Mr. Lockwood said "the Corporation expressed no opinion" on the matter, apparently meaning that the Greenrock Corporation, as well as the realty company, chose to stay out of the library matter.

This was a little too much for Mrs. Coombs to accept, especially after Town Supervisor Parsons became irritated with her for making "trouble" and raising questions about Rockefeller taxes in relation to library assessments. If only seven people in the whole district objected to the project, after an extensive promotion campaign, and if neither the Rockefellers nor the three major corporations who pay 90 per cent of the district's taxes *didn't* object—as they declared they did not—then who kept Pocantico Hills off the tax rolls while every other district in the town had to foot the bills? And how did that law for the exclusion of Pocantico Hills get through the State Legislature?

"Why is everybody so secretive and furtive?" asked Mrs. Coombs at one public forum. "Why do Town officeholders say one thing one day and another thing the next day? The only reasonable answer to the puzzle seems to be that this Town of Mount Pleasant is being run principally for the benefit of the Rockefellers.

"I agree that the Rockefeller family has been a great benefactor of the arts, medicine, the United Nations and so on, but they seem to be frugal, misleading, and dictatorial as Mount Pleasant neighbors.

". . . if the Rockefeller property were properly assessed, Town taxes would be reduced twenty per cent and [our] share of county taxes would be reduced ten per cent. Mount Pleasant is a big town now, not a feudal estate. . . . Thousands of families whose last name is not Rockefeller live here."

148

This sort of material, with its direct criticism of the Rockefeller interests, was more than a little shocking to people who read it in *The Tarrytown Daily News,* which calls itself Governor Rockefeller's "hometown newspaper." It tends to be sugary in its news columns when reporting on the Rockefellers, and unbearably profuse with praise on its editorial page.

The Pocantico Hills School District seems to lead a charmed life in still another respect. Throughout New York State, and indeed throughout much of the United States, state and federal pressure has been exerted on local school districts to merge educational facilities, making available to students special academic opportunities that are neither economically nor physically possible in smaller districts.

All around the Pocantico Hills district, merger plans are afoot under the prodding of both necessity and the State Education Department. But the district of the Rockefellers, with its extraordinarily low taxes, high assessments, and low student population, has not been asked by the State to merge with any adjoining district. No district exists which could combine with Pocantico Hills without increasing the latter's taxes.

Every year proposals are put before the Mount Pleasant Town Board urging public trash and garbage collections— one of the routine services taxpayers provide for themselves through sanitation departments or health laws in nearly every urban and suburban area. No such modern fads have come to the unincorporated districts of the Town of Mount Pleasant, where those who want their trash collected pay a monthly contract rate to private disposal companies. Because of the concentration of wealth in the area where the Rockefeller estate takes care of its own garbage disposal problems, public removal of trash would mean that

Pocantico Hills would have to pay about 20 per cent of the cost. Thus no action on this service considered elsewhere essential has yet been taken.

Much of the property in unincorporated township lands of Westchester County, and elsewhere in the state for that matter, is assigned to sewer districts, sometimes even when the assigned property is not within range of any public sewage disposal lines. Disgruntled citizens have been known to complain to the Town Board that a good deal of Rockefeller land seems to be unassigned to any sewer district and simultaneously free of any sewer tax assessments. Unfortunately, most complaints of this nature are traced to people who admit they are Democrats, which permits the local government to reject the complaints as invalid because they are "politically" inspired.

Another tax advantage that accrues to Rockefeller land operations has a somewhat ironic coloration to it. The Greenrock Corporation, which in itself provides certain tax considerations not available under individually reported tax returns, has become the legalism by which the Governor, who personally pushed the state sales tax into law, apparently doesn't have to pay it.

Under the sales tax law, the levy is collected from the ultimate consumer. Corporations which purchase goods for resale do not, of course, pay the tax, nor do certain exempt enterprises, such as a farm, pay sales taxes on equipment or supplies needed to operate the place. When Greenrock makes purchases required in the management and operation of the Rockefeller estate, sales tax exemption can be claimed under control No. 13-1929826, which is the control number assigned by the State Department of Taxation and Finance to the company owned by Nelson and his brothers.

It is not clear whether this beneficial exemption from

state sales taxes is legal in the case of the Greenrock Corporation, which is wholly owned by the Rockefellers and which is a corporate device to manage estate property. There is no evidence that Greenrock sells at retail anything it purchases, in which case legitimate exemption could be claimed and sales taxes paid by the buyer to Greenrock, which would then in turn transmit the tax collections to the appropriate state agency. Inquiries to several state officials about the Rockefeller exemption from the sales tax produced a nervous, even agitated, response, but none was willing to try to confirm the assignment of Control Number 13-1929826 to the Greenrock Corporation.

A former legislator, who knows his way around in Albany and who was able to reach the proper source in the State Department of Taxation and Finance, did confirm the facts as they are understood and published here for the first time. Oddly enough, John D. Rockefeller's Fieldwood Farm could probably qualify for sales tax exemption under the law, but so far as it could be determined, the farm has not done so. It appears that John does not get the tax discount, or ask for it, in purchases that could be confirmed.

Just as estate property can be classified as farmland, with thousands of acres taxed at a fraction of the rate paid by owners of one or two acres, so can a large landholder, operating as a corporation, buy sickle bars and tractors at one price, if he qualifies for exemption, while the small landowner's equipment, even if it is identical equipment, costs him that added "2 per cent for Rocky" that merchants' tax collection containers refer to.

No analysis of the extent or amount of purchases made by Greenrock, which of course does not buy for resale, has thus far been possible, since purchases are not correlated with tax-exemption numbers. State Comptroller Arthur Levitt's office has reported that there is no way to determine the extent of Greenrock purchases, or exactly what merchandise was exempted from the sales tax. Personal visitations to the State Comptroller's office in Albany elicited no response on this matter and Mr. Levitt himself would not answer mail on the subject.

The several hundred families whose properties share common boundaries with the great estate, or who look upon it in their commuting and shopping travels around it, have a special affection for the Rockefellers—a kind of tenacious loyalty rooted in an instinctive understanding of what makes a property valuable. To own or live on a bit of land that looks out on this kingdom of open space, thirty-five to forty minutes from Grand Central Terminal along one of the most spectacularly beautiful commuting rides on earth; to be physically near this green island of natural splendor, set in an urban world against which an inexorable tide of growth and congestion is pressing, is recognized as an unpurchasable treasure measured on a scale of diminishing months and years. Everything within sight or range of its influence is affected by the presence of the great estate.

On a magnificent slope of 360 acres, overlooking the River, about halfway between the Rockefeller estate and the town of Ossining, is the Sleepy Hollow Country Club at Scarborough-on-Hudson. With two golf courses, three riding rings—one of them indoors—and seventy-five miles of Rockefeller trails extending outward in all directions from the stable gate, it is probably the finest place in the Northeast to hold a club membership for those whose favorite sport is horseback riding.

The main house of the Club is another of those great ornate Hudson River mansions built toward the end of the nineteenth century. The building was designed by architect Stanford White, who was shot to death in the old Madison

Square Garden restaurant in 1906 by Harry K. Thaw, after the latter heard White was philandering with his wife. The house was built for Colonel Eliott Fitch Shepard, who married into the Vanderbilt millions, and who died shortly after it was occupied. In 1911 it became a country club and several Rockefellers have held membership in it. The Club has remained more socially pretentious than exclusive, but for many years it was anti-Semitic in its membership limitations (as, indeed, were many other clubs of similar vintage). A few years ago, word was passed down from the Rockefellers—through channels that avoided any distressing personal confrontations between the family and Club officials—that anti-Semitism was no longer to be tolerated.

It was rather a blow to a good many of the 425 or so members of the Club, but there was no official opposition to the suggestion that the membership rules be adjusted to conform to the Rockefeller requirements. It was said, in defense of the Club's past history on the matter, that one Jew *had* been a member for quite a long time. He was Major Bowes, who had made a fortune in the old radio Amateur Hour productions, and his membership was considered to be a special case, scarcely a violation of the code that disallowed Jews. When Major Bowes died and left a hefty piece of his fortune to Francis Cardinal Spellman and the New York Archdiocese, no replacement Jewish membership was allowed, and the club clung to its simon-pure principle which the presence of Major Bowes had not measurably sullied.

The onetime membership of Major Bowes was not enough to obliterate its taint of anti-Semitism, and the Club was obliged to liberalize its membership if it wanted to retain the official good will of the Rockefeller family, who no longer tolerated such nonsense—especially if it threatened to become a public issue. The Club capitulated and there was some discreet scurrying about on the part of its Membership Committee, selecting the correct number and the kind of Jews to show compliance with the desegregation order, but at the same time not putting the Club in the position of overdoing it. The president of a major tobacco company who owned a nearby estate, and the president of a New York textile firm agreed to join to get the Club off the hook. The tobacco company president became a member to do the Club a favor more than anything else, and scarcely ever puts in an appearance at the place.

In any case, the Club marched manfully into the twentieth century and it cannot be said that anti-Semitism prevails any longer as a policy, notwithstanding the fact that after the desegregation order was complied with, few other instances of liberalized ethnic representation were reported. But the quiet word—scarcely more than a nod to the auctioneer from a prestigious collector—altered a rigid policy that had stood for two generations. There are Jews today in the Sleepy Hollow Club and the Rockefeller magic accomplished it.

Changes more profound than the question of who is privileged to join country clubs are in the making at the estate. No landholdings of the size and value of the Rockefellers' can remain open space indefinitely, and none of this size and worth have lasted this long. It is not a matter of whether it will remain a stable barony, with new lands added from time to time, but how soon and under what circumstances the greatest body of land in the New York metropolitan area will be converted to commercial enterprises, development, and—money.

What saved the Tarrytown area from becoming, in all probability, a full-sized city with no more open land than an occasional convent or untaxed institution could hang onto, was John D. Rockefeller's money. For many years, virtually every piece of property that became available was purchased by the Rockefellers if at some point it touched the family's lands. Villages and communities spread outward until they reached a Rockefeller boundary and there the development stopped. It was a form of zoning imposed on communities that often allows real estate interests to determine the extent and quality of growth, which is why it is generally unplanned and quite bad.

Significant signs that great plans are afoot for the development and use of estate lands have cropped up more often in recent years. After World War II, John D. Rockefeller, Jr., tried to have the United Nations locate on the estate grounds and offered the international body large tracts of land as a gift. An opportunity to create a new city, a kind of modern American Geneva, was lost when the preference for Manhattan as the home for the UN won over other contenders. The Rockefellers were donors of the land for the United Nations buildings anyway, having quickly arranged to acquire and contribute the site when it appeared the UN might take its debating and peacemaking business elsewhere.

When Dwight D. Eisenhower, while waiting to become President of the United States, was president of Columbia University, there were discussions among leaders of The Establishment on the long-range prospects of relocating part of Columbia on the Rockefeller lands in the later years of the twentieth century. It is quite likely that this project is reviewed from time to time.

Columbia University is the landlord of the Rockefellers by virtue of the fact that it has leased to the family the site on which Rockefeller Center stands. John D., Jr., first leased midtown lots from Columbia as early as 1928, when he had hopes of bringing the Metropolitan Opera into a great new home on Sixth Avenue, across the street from what is now Radio City Music Hall. The Metropolitan, divided by jealousies, temperamental indecision, and a lingering love for its old baroque opera house just off Times Square, stayed where it was. Finally, however, the Metropolitan Opera is now moving uptown, thirty-seven years after the Rockefellers' original invitation was declined. The Met will go into the new Lincoln Center complex, which Rockefeller planning and money were, in a large measure, responsible for developing. Irreverent complaints that the Rockefellers were using their influence and vast resources at Lincoln Center to put together an enormous cultural supermarket this time did not halt or even appreciably slow down the largest project of its kind the world has ever seen.

The lease which Columbia University holds on Rockefeller Center was modified in 1953, with terms stipulated until 1973 and options to the year 2,069. Lease modifications which Laurance S. Rockefeller signed for the family in 1953 are under renegotiation and review in 1966, and there is some speculative feeling that something important, massive, and expensive is in the planning stage. For when the lease expires on Rockefeller Center, all of the property and improvements revert to Columbia University. The Rockefellers undoubtedly would like to have another great operation in full bloom then—perhaps more than one. The $125 million put into Rockefeller Center has doubtless increased in value, after thirty-five years, how many times? Three, four, five? Value to whom and for what?

Through the years, the Rockefellers have failed in their attempts to close off or curtail traffic on Route 117, the old Bedford Road which divides the estate like a blacktop ribbon. Underpasses and bridges had to be built by the Rockefellers to diminish the divisive effect of the road and

156

to bring unity to the estate lands. But what could not be done by economic power and courteous persuasion, might now be done with gubernatorial power, for Governor Rockefeller is determined to have a new Route 117 at a new place. Whatever the merits of a new route, or lack of them, the little road through the estate does not appear to have much of a future. The new multiple lane highway across the land could have an enormous bearing on what happens to the old Sleepy Hollow countryside which Rockefeller ownership has protected and preserved through most of this century.

Engineering and architectural firms have been engaged by the Rockefellers to do survey and planning studies which, privately paid for or not, are likely to have public repercussions in the near and long-range future. The John Clarkson engineering firm is said to have made road-building and engineering studies, and it is known that even the engineers of the regional office of the State Department of Public Works were kept in the dark on matters that are routinely within its jurisdiction.

In the past year, surveyors' crews have been studying the countryside in the old Sleepy Hollow country north of Tarrytown while, concurrently, engineers and workmen have been making borings of the river bottom and shore line along the east bank of the Hudson. The work along the river's edge is, of course, preliminary to the construction of a wide, limited access expressway, while the crews working inland have been making site preparations for the Rockefeller Spur, as it is called. Bright orange marker pennants have appeared, tied to trees and shrubbery, along the route of the new public right-of-way to cross the Rockefeller estate at its northern end.

The presence of the telltale pennants was the first visible evidence of the road Governor Rockefeller insists upon,

157

but which other members of the Rockefeller family "bitterly" oppose. Nelson confessed that "some of the members of my family are bitterly opposed to this" in February of 1966 when he summoned a thousand or so participants to the Governor's Conference on Natural Beauty at the Hilton Hotel in New York.

He was greeted at the Conference, which he called three years after it was authorized by the State Legislature in 1963, by a dozen or so pickets, all residents and neighbors from the Pocantico Hills and Tarrytown area. They carried signs protesting the new highway and denouncing it as a contradiction to "natural beauty."

Mr. Rockefeller, acknowledging the protests, told the press he had "no choice but to support the recommendations of the State Department of Public Works." It was more likely that the "choice" to construct the new road originated with the Rockefellers inasmuch as they have been trying unsuccessfully for at least thirty-five years to close off Route 117. The New York press reported charges that the Rockefeller Spur was designed primarily to get some of the estate acreage rezoned for industrial use. The loyal Gannett newspapers in Westchester County printed an account of proposals made at the Conference on Natural Beauty, but made no mention of the Tarrytown contingent picketing it. Governor Rockefeller, in acknowledging that members of his family were disturbed by the highway projects, said he had no intention of rezoning or selling estate property.

It would be quite possible to plan building, industrial, and commercial developments on two to three thousand acres of estate land that would produce, in the century that lies ahead, more money for Rockefeller descendants, heirs, and families—and for Rockefeller foundations, research institutions, and charities—than Rockefeller Center itself

158

has ever brought into the family coffers. It is not only possible, but something along this line is likely.

The Rockefeller family is necessarily preoccupied with money. An adviser once told the founder of the fortune that effective means had to be found to dispose of it or it would "crush" those who possessed it. This old counsel is perennially true. The need to find new ways by which an increasing fortune can be put to use exerts pressure on Rockefeller interests, and unquestionably produces as many problems as wealth itself solves. But the ownership of 3,668 acres of precious and largely vacant land that fronts onto an open channel to the oceans, and that adjoins fast expressways leading to the nation's markets, provides unparalleled opportunities to put Rockefeller money to new, bold, and possibly grandiose uses.

Beginning in the late 1950s, large tracts of estate lands, which had been classified as undeveloped farm land and small acre plots, were rezoned in some areas for housing, industrial, and commercial use. The Town of Mount Pleasant had zoned the acreage along Bedford Road for small businesses, a supermarket and other retail operations to service a community of twenty one thousand people. These plans would be pointless if the Governor succeeds in building a new expressway to replace Bedford Road. But the private projects which the Rockefellers have on the drawing boards for the use of their land may make a great deal of public community planning in the lower Hudson Valley obsolete. The architectural firm of I. M. Pei & Associates is rumored to be on the Rockefeller payroll to work on ideas for the future of the area.

If the family which owns the land has, among its other assets, enormous capital of its own, the resources of great banking and investment institutions, the governorship of

New York State, influence over state agencies and scores of foundations and conservation organizations, and the determined will to do things on a grand scale, the United States may see an estate converted into a planners' dream of a newly created industrial and residential city of the future.

Land which John and William Rockefeller bought before this century began is priceless in the precise meaning of the word, for the reason that so little of such land is left. How much would fresh water or clean air be worth if there were not enough to go around? This is becoming the measure and the value of open land in the cityscape of the most congested part of America. And it is what the Rockefellers, in addition to their many other dubious blessings, possess. One gives the land away or keeps it for investment use. On such land, new fortunes can be amassed as long as the urban world remains with us. It doesn't take computers to prove that growth and development, if they do not destroy or demean urban life to the point of unendurability, are continuing at an explosive rate. Barring such miracles as instant, if not total, birth control and a sudden, acceptable, nontoxic space-saving substitute for the automobile, most of us are doomed to spend our lives in increasing numbers on diminishing ground space. More and more highways will be built, a hundred million new automobiles will be disgorged from U.S. factories in the next ten years, and individuals will be scrounging for air to breathe, water to drink, and house room to live in. It is not possible for large land areas presently unoccupied, green and open, to remain as they are. Too much ready money and too little civilized restraint produce a dynamism of urban ruination called progress.

If $4,000 a year per acre can be realized on 80 per cent of the Rockefeller land, leaving the remaining seven hundred acres in family residential use, by the end of the century—which is in less time than the Rockefellers have owned Rockefeller Center—an income of $12 million a year on land leases alone would be collected, exclusive of any income derived from enterprises to which the land might be devoted.

The government of Westchester County, under the one-man direction of County Executive Edwin G. Michaelian, maintains a hands-off policy where Rockefeller interests are concerned. Mr. Michaelian, Governor Rockefeller, and the leader of his legislative troops, Lieutenant Governor Malcolm Wilson, understand each other to the extent that no objections can be expected from the county government on Rockefeller plans for expressway construction, at public expense, or estate land development at private expense, to give the Pocantico territory its highest possible value. Only occasional grumbling is heard in the State Legislature about the use of Rockefeller economic, political, and gubernatorial power to surround his estate lands with expressways, to be paid for with state and federal funds, on the grounds it would provide traffic convenience to nearby communities.

The nearby communities, in expressions made both by citizens and made officially by local governments, have become angered and horrified at the "traffic convenience" Governor Rockefeller seeks to impose upon them in order to serve his own long-term ends. The government of Mount Pleasant, following public hearings, in 1966 upzoned tracts of Rockefeller land holdings in the face of strenuous objections from the estate. It was an act of retaliation against the Rockefellers for the Governor's threat to build expressways that would undoubtedly bring ultimate industrialization and congestion to the last large tract of open countryside in the lower Hudson Valley.

7

Rockefeller as Highwayman:
THE HUDSON EXPRESSWAY SCANDAL

In early 1966, the Citizens Committee for the Hudson Valley submitted a legal brief to all New York State Senators and Assemblymen out of which one paragraph leaps with a grave charge. The brief urges the repeal of one of Governor Rockefeller's pet projects, the building of an expressway along the east shore of the Hudson River and a spur just north of Pocantico Hills. Referring to the spur, the crucial paragraph states:

One major effect is to provide at public expense future access to large land areas *controlled by a single interest* * for the development of enormous concentrations of shopper complexes and residential communities, and it is repectfully urged, again, that a thorough study be made of the traffic needs of this area before committing public funds to a project which appears at first blush, to be entirely unnecessary and of dubious purpose.

The "single interest" is Nelson Rockefeller. And the import of this paragraph is that the Governor of the State of New York jammed through his legislature a bill involving the expenditure of several hundred millions of dollars of public funds to build unneeded roads which will add millions to the value of his personal property.

The story behind this scandal is a singular demonstra-

* Emphasis added.

tion of the avarice of the very rich, and reveals with striking clarity the moral values and political machinations by which Nelson Rockefeller chooses to run his State as he works his way toward the Presidency. Moreover, to grasp fully the facts about the highway scandal is to understand how Rockefeller acts when there is a sharp conflict between the public interest and his own.

Broadway, one of the best known streets in the world, wends its way through the great length of Manhattan Island and then north through the Bronx and on up, slightly inland from the Hudson River, through Westchester County and counties further north, where, for most of its way, it is known as the Albany Post Road, for it does indeed go all the way to Albany. It is the route along which mail was carried by stagecoach to the State Capitol. The Albany Post Road cuts through many towns on the east bank of the Hudson River and in two creates something of a bottleneck during periods of peak use. The first is Tarrytown, in the Sleepy Hollow country of Washington Irving, which Governor Rockefeller now calls his home town. The second is Ossining, where the Sing Sing Indians gave their name to what is now the most famous prison in the United States. While the rush-hour traffic jams in Ossining and Tarrytown are nowhere near as formidable as they are in New York City, they are a substantial nuisance both for through travelers and local residents; the latter have long advocated building bypasses around both towns. It is the need for these two bypasses which has been overblown into Nelson Rockefeller's most expensive folly, the Hudson River Expressway and Spur which according to Burch McMorran, Rockefeller's obedient Superintendent of Public Works, would cost $188,000,000, and, according to other estimates, far more.

Why is Rockefeller so anxious to spend so many tens

163

of millions of taxpayer dollars for a highway which would further despoil the Hudson River Valley when all that's needed are bypasses around two towns? And why would Rockefeller jam enabling legislation through the Senate and Assembly in Albany for a highway complex that the road builders favor and the people don't?

The suspicions of people living all along the Hudson River Valley were first aroused by the way in which the two bills for the Hudson Expressway and the Rockefeller Spur were passed into law. In May of 1965, the two bills were suddenly put before the legislature in a deliberately vague form. The route numbers were obscure designations taken from Department of Public Works maps which the legislators—or laymen—could not be familiar with. The draftsman was not identified. The three readings required by law were deliberately telescoped. The bills passed without debate or question, and for the most part without any knowledge on the part of the lawmakers of what they were actually voting for. The normal chaos of the closing days of the legislative session prevailed. The bills appeared to be routine legislation to permit the State Department of Public Works to study highway extension. However, the second bill, referring to roadways in Westchester county, did arouse the suspicion of Assemblyman Lawrence A. Cabot, serving his first term in the Assembly. Cabot represented a Hudson Valley district which adjoins but does not include the Rockefeller estate. When the bill was called up for a vote, Cabot in turn called for a delay. He ducked out from the Assembly floor to telephone district headquarters of the Department of Public Works at Poughkeepsie, New York, which has jurisdiction in the lower Hudson Valley. Nobody at Poughkeepsie knew a thing about the legislation or any plans for highway construction along the Hudson.

164

Suspicious but still incredulous, Cabot got in touch with the State DPW headquarters at Albany, which had sent the two bills through the Rules Committee to the Legislature but which had concealed a vital fact from both the Senate and the Assembly. Normally, a DPW bill is identified by the statement: *"This bill was prepared under the direction of the New York State Department of Public Works and was introduced at its request."* This statement was not included. At the same time, each bill is routinely accompanied by a memorandum explaining in precise terms what new highway mileage is intended and designating the specific areas, right down to street corners, that are to be affected. None of this information, in fact no memorandum at all, was offered.

The Albany office told Cabot that the localities affected by the proposed new roads had "requested" the bills. Cabot knew this was a lie. Time was running out and he had to get back quickly to the Assembly and try to obtain additional delay. Cabot, who is a Democrat, had a quick conference with Assemblyman Richard Cerosky, a Republican representing the Rockefeller estate district, who was equally confounded by the bills which both men knew would raise havoc among their constituents. Both voted against the Expressway Bill—the only two negative votes recorded in the Assembly.

The moment parliamentary rules permitted, Cabot requested the Assembly Speaker Anthony Travia—Mayor Wagner's key man and Governor Rockefeller's accomplice of the moment—to recall the Expressway Bill. Travia announced that the bill had already been dispatched by courier to Governor Rockefeller, who was waiting at his Manhattan office on 55th Street for it.

The following day the other bill, authorizing a 3.5 mile connecting road from the Hudson River area in North

Tarrytown to main north-south arteries feeding into New York City, was passed with the same two dissenting votes. Shortly thereafter the legislative session ended. Governor Rockefeller, with the acquiescence of his helpmate, J. Burch McMorran, whom he had appointed to the job of superintendent of the State Department of Public Works, had legalized an expressway project that would:

1. Cost a minimum of a quarter of a billion dollars, with every likelihood that accesses and connecting links into New York City would add an additional hundred million.

2. Convert the waterfront areas of the Hudson River into an expendable, sprawling corridor, eliminating any future chance of reclaiming and rehabilitating a shoreline that a century of neglect and abuse had blighted.

3. Enormously enhance the value of Rockefeller lands.

4. Violate the planning and zoning ordinances of every community it traversed.

5. Remove from taxation a swath of land which, with grading, might average 350 to 400 feet in width in every village and town it bisected.

6. Condemn to destruction property ranging in character from slums and small, middle-class homes and businesses, to costly residences on exclusive riverside slopes which, even if saved, would be virtually worthless beside a six- or eight-lane expressway.

7. Fail to solve the problem of local traffic congestion and therefore necessitate other highway expansion preferable in the first place.

The ruinous characteristic of the Hudson Expressway Bill was not the fact that it was another "scenic" commercial truck route, but that it specifically designated the alignment of the roadway in a narrow corridor regardless of other traffic and community considerations. The law located the expressway in a ribbon of land between the river's edge and the old Albany Post Road, which extends from lower Manhattan to Albany. This corridor in some areas is a few hundred feet to a half mile wide.

It would accomplish, at a dreadful cost, what Governor Rockefeller declared was of great value: truckers and tourists could drive at sixty-mile-an-hour speeds while observing the panoramic views of the Hudson River. Further, he argued, it would allow "more people" in this motoring fashion to see the Hudson Valley from their cars. He felt it would be a great tourist attraction.

Mr. Rockefeller seemed unable to distinguish between a tourist attraction that carried motorists through butchered up corridors from which people would have to be ejected, and the grandeur of a rehabilitated riverscape closed to streaming traffic, yet providing access to the river at a multitude of places in which solace, beauty, quiet, and absence of automobile fumes would be welcome.

It is not only in Rockefeller's New York but throughout the nation that the power of the roadbuilders is increasing steadily. Private roadbuilders make money out of building highways—the bigger the better—not out of discussing the pros and cons, or even the necessity, of a given roadway. They are locked in a marriage of will and intent with men in government who work ostensibly for the people but who actually derive their satisfaction not from serving the public interest but from building more and more roads. Government highway authorities exercise their enormous power in uprooting communities, dislocating families, condemning businesses, and sending them all running, refugees from their own environment, in order to make way for the paved expanses that take priority over other human and commercial needs. The authorities and engineers who lay out routes love, above all things, limited accesses, straight lines and high speed, and many human values are sacrificed to these ingredients of traffic mobility.

Studies are conducted, whirring computers digest programmed tapes and spew forth projections of where, on the basis of population growth and economic expansion, new highways will be built, and those new roadways are normally sketched in advance on highway department maps so that people may know where the next lands will be consumed, the next roadside business opportunities opened up, and the next shortcuts around congested towns may be possible. There are nearly 85 million vehicles owned by Americans and their businesses, with a hundred million men and women operating them. And in the next ten years it is likely that another hundred million will be spun off the assembly lines and onto the crowded roads, the incredibly packed streets, into the noxious air, the superhighways, and littered countryside—if, indeed, there is any countryside left when this geometric progression of population, combustion engines, asphalt-covered earth, sulphuric particulants and homosecticides reach a full measure of expression.

The automobile has not only come to dominate the human scale, it is wedded to it in a fusion of necessity. It is a prior condition of urban life, an extension—in the sobering imagery of Constantinos Doxiades, a Greek urban planner and designer of international reputation— of the mythological centaur. We have become men who are not, like the centaur, half horse and half human, but half man and half car, immobile beyond pedestrian limits without our gaseous engines fueled, our lubricious bearings turning, brake drums beating to the rhythm of the sounding horn, our clutch automatic, our exact currency flipped into the thank-you chute and our origin-and-destination tattooed onto the punch card for the Great Changemaker at the end of the road.

When general outrage about Rockefeller's new Expressway mounted to a virtual storm, the Governor tried to deflect the criticism by making public a letter he had written to J. Burch McMorran, to whom the new law gave authority to proceed with engineering studies and construction of the road at will. (This is the same McMorran who withheld required information and accompanying memoranda from the legislators, and had concealed the fact that the expressway legislation originated in his office.) The Governor "requested" Mr. McMorran to follow certain suggestions in building the riverfront expressway.

It would be nice, the Governor thought, if Mr. McMorran would "consider" constructing a walkway along the inner, or river, edge of the speedway; a kind of concrete sidewalk which cyclists and pedestrians could reach through underpasses or over bridges. Benches should be installed, too, so that people could cross over or under the fenced-in superhighway and sit with their books to the roaring diesels while looking at the river and the scenic valley.

Newly formed citizens groups on both sides of the Hudson besieged President Johnson, Senator Jacob Javits, and Senator Robert F. Kennedy with complaints urging their intervention. The President expressed the hope, in one of his television appearances, that both the Hudson and the Potomac River could be cleaned up and their shorelines, what remained of them, preserved for future generations. One congressman observed that both rivers were so choked with garbage that it wouldn't take much of a "miracle" to walk across them.

Senator Kennedy assigned a staff member to research

the New York State legislation and joined with Senator Javits, his Republican senatorial colleague from New York, in offering a bill in the Senate what was very much like a bill which Congressman Richard Ottinger, who had opposed Rockefeller in the Con Ed matter, had introduced in the House.

Senator Javits dispatched a letter to Rockefeller that demanded an answer. He raised questions about the expressway in a manner that clearly indicated he had been under pressure from a multitude of complaints. The Governor made public his written response, in which he defended the road as essential along the alignment designated, and bluntly brushed off the protesting constituents as "idiotic and politically motivated."

Seven villages in the lower Hudson Valley authorized their mayors to fight the Rockefeller project with its threat of wiping out their riverfront areas. The mayors, representing communities from the Yonkers line to the Croton-on-Hudson boundary, made public some untidy facts about the way they had been "betrayed" by J. Burch McMorran and the Rockefeller administrative staff. Four of the mayors —from Ossining, Briarcliff Manor, North Tarrytown, and Tarrytown—had long been concerned about state plans for providing local traffic relief in bottleneck areas, particularly through the business districts of Ossining and The Tarrytowns. The mayors had sought an audience with the Governor in the spring of 1965 to recommend local bypass roads to relieve village traffic conditions and to improve the wide right-of-way of parallel Route 9A. Both rights-of-way are already the property of the state except where the Albany Post Road serves as village streets. No one asked for the riverfront expressway nor would any mayor have countenanced it.

The Governor did not bother to answer the mayors'

requests, but his executive aide and cousin, Alexander Aldrich, wrote to inform them that J. Burch McMorran was being "requested" to supply the latest information and that the Governor was interested in their local problems. The mayors' request for a meeting with him was ignored.

McMorran wrote to the four mayors in a letter postmarked May 25 saying that new legislation had been introduced for a Hudson Expressway and that the district engineers from Poughkeepsie would get in touch with them. *The fact was that the bill already had been passed when McMorran's letter was mailed.* Repeated assurance over past years that the villages would be consulted in connection with highway plans affecting their towns were dishonored by Rockefeller.

Not only were the district engineers at Poughkeepsie unaware of legislation creating a massive new highway in their area of jurisdiction, but Laurance Rockefeller and Conrad L. Wirth and every member of the Hudson River Valley Commission, which Nelson had hastily appointed, were in complete ignorance of the project until they read about it in the press. Conrad Wirth, Executive Director of the Commission, told a delegation which visited his office in Rockefeller Center that he personally read of the expressway along the river he was supposed to "study" while he was on a boat excursion in the Hudson, presumably making preliminary observations, four days after the bill passed the Legislature. Governor Rockefeller had neither informed nor consulted with the commission he established to help decide the fate and future of the Hudson Valley.

There were other disclosures. McMorran named a precise $188 million as the cost of building the road from Beacon to New York City, but he said no one knew precisely where the route would be within the confines of the corridor designated. No borings had been made in the river, yet McMorran said the expressway might be built over water for 20 to 30 per cent of the distance. When he was asked what traffic studies had been made and what origin-and-destination data had been compiled for traffic expected to use the expressway, it developed that *no such material existed.*

McMorran made further pronouncements that sections of the expressway would be built over the New York Central tracks—as had once been proposed in the 1930s. The New York Central was excited at the prospects of millions of dollars in cash for the sale of air rights, but announcement of the passage of legislation to build the expressway was as surprising to railroad management executives as it was to members of the Hudson River Valley Commission.

Although the expressway was expected to carry long-distance traffic, as well as any local traffic that could get to it, southward to the Riverdale section of The Bronx, then over condemned land and apartment house complexes, through congested residential areas that would have to be ripped out, to connect with the New York State Thruway north of Manhattan, *not a single official of New York City had heard a word about the expressway legislation.* The New York City Planning Commission was aghast, and several of its members were caustically critical in private but made no public comment until a Congressional committee hearing was held later in the summer.

In Washington, Congressman Richard L. Ottinger cried foul. Stewart Udall, Secretary of the Interior, who had told Laurance his department would withhold calling for unilateral federal action on the Hudson until it could be determined what New York's own plans might be, was dismayed. A fifty-five-mile expressway along the riverfront left little for either the Hudson River Valley Commission or Congress or the Department of the Interior to study, insofar as one side of the lower valley was concerned. It was understood that Udall, who had long been on a first-name basis with the Rockefellers, was cool and concerned over the roadway project. Udall and Ottinger got together, Ottinger asked for help from the Congressional Committee on Interior and Insular Affairs, and plans were made to hold subcommittee hearings in the Hudson Valley on Ottinger's proposed federal legislation.

J. Burch McMorran would see neither the mayors nor any other authorities who were vigorously protesting the project. The estimate of $188 million for the expressway was plainly ludicrous, in that no feasibility studies had been made and no plans for specifically aligning the road had been considered. Authoritative estimates on the cost of the road ran from a high of twelve million dollars a mile if built over the water at the river's edge; eight million dollars a mile over the railroad tracks; more than that if built on fill dumped into the river, and anywhere from four to six million dollars a mile if cut into the rock bluffs and laid out parallel to the New York Central tracks.

Legislators are subject to severe criticism and, often, reprisals when proposals affecting the voters in their districts are enacted into law. Lawrence A. Cabot and Richard Cerosky in the Assembly and Senators Bernard Gordon of Peekskill and Royden Letsen of Yonkers represented the Hudson River area threatened by the Governor's new highway. Cabot and Letsen were Democrats; Cerosky and Gordon, Republicans. All were against the expressway legislation, although Senator Letsen voted for the project, to his subsequent horror, on the assumption that it was a routine departmental study bill. Another senator, Max Berking, representing the Long Island Sound area at Rye, terminus of a six-and-a-half mile bridge proposed by the autocratic Robert Moses of New York City, was similarly deceived by the expressway bill. He, too, thought it was a study bill and that his simple senatorial courtesy vote was expected. When he learned he had voted for an unwanted expressway along the Hudson, he said, "I have been deluded. I am ashamed."

The shame was really Rockefeller's. It was he who had the bills railroaded through an unsuspecting Legislature.

While Republicans Cerosky and Gordon, in deference to their outraged constituents, voted against the legislation, their opposition ended at that point because both are part of the Rockefeller—Michaelian establishment in Westchester. While mild objections were permissible as appropriate expressions of sympathy for their unhappy constituents, no active opposition to Governor Rockefeller or to Westchester County Executive Edwin Michaelian is tolerated. The Governor is the state's principal contributor to the Republican Party and is generous with campaign contributions to any Republican nominee, particularly if the nominee faces strong opposition. Mr. Rockefeller has spent a good many millions of dollars trying to be President and is quite prepared to spend millions more, but he expects answering loyalty from his beneficiaries. Money talks, even if what it exacts is silence.

Lawrence Cabot, motivated both by political interest and personal curiosity, has tried to find out the extent of Rockefeller financial support and so have many others. Through a process of "loans" to local, city, town, county, and state Republican committees, plus contributions to individual candidates, plus financial assistance to dozens of "committees" established to spend money then dissolve, the financing of a political party eludes inquiry and research by techniques of concealment not entirely dissimilar from those prevailing in Cosa Nostra. Both Republican and Democratic parties adhere to equally evasive, arcane practices in covering the tracks of money, but the Republican Party, because it seems to attract the larger contributors generally, has refined the system especially well.

Cabot arrived at an educated guess as to what Nelson Rockefeller might have contributed to Republican elections in New York State. One day in the Assembly, several Republican legislators were grumbling aloud about Mr. Rockefeller's iron-fisted tactics in pushing the state sales tax through the Assembly. The Republicans were expected to cast their votes without too much argument, even though their upstate constituents were overwhelmingly against the measure.

"Why do you put up with it?" Cabot asked. "Why not vote against the bill?"

As Cabot explained their response, "They looked at me kind of uncomprehendingly, and one of them said, 'Now look, Larry, anyone of us can be reapportioned out of office. You're a Democrat, right? Now, if it was a Democratic governor and you were told you could have help with your campaign financing, and he put six hundred thousand dollars a year into the party campaign fund, and I'm only talking about the state, mind you, not the country . . . well, what would you do?' " *

In the historic Tarrytown area, revulsion against the expressway was intensified by the authorization of the 3.5 mile Rockefeller Spur that would connect the expressway with roads to the east. The background has to be understood to grasp the reasons for the outrage. At present,

* The use of Rockefeller money in his personal operations and in the Republican Party is screened by the very complexity of his official and family connections. Private airplanes and motor vehicles can be deflected to party work, and they are; family personnel can be assigned, and is, to party headquarters—and none of it shows up in expenditures.

175

Route 117, a fairly quiet country road, cuts through the huge Rockefeller holdings on an east-west line. This is the road that, for much of its length, is bounded by inhospitable high fences. The Rockefellers would like to get rid of this public road entirely. Therefore, the Rockefeller Spur, which is to traverse approximately the same distance, but further north, would "replace" the bothersome Route 117 with a superhighway that would run adjacent to the more remote northern section of the Rockefeller holdings. The fact that the new superhighway would dislocate Rockefeller neighbors, who cherish their homes in this beautiful section of Westchester, doesn't seem to bother the Governor at all. Nor is he troubled with the cost of building this superhighway, for which there is clearly no present need and will not be until such time that Rockefeller or his heirs decide to develop the northern parts of their huge property.

While the Gannett newspapers poured forth an almost daily hymn of praise to the Governor and urged him to build both the expressway and the spur with all possible haste, the mayor of Tarrytown, Anthony Veteran, a stocky, plain-spoken man unawed by the nearby presence of the Rockefeller estate, demanded public hearings on the matter and charged that the river roadway would wipe out years of planning and development.

Mr. Veteran, who is principal of Alexander Hamilton High School in the nearby village of Elmsford as well as mayor of Tarrytown, denounced the expressway legislation as "a crass abuse of gubernatorial power by Mr. Rockefeller, whose own lands stand to increase in value by millions of dollars while Hudson River communities are cut to pieces, while taxable properties are wiped out and all life irreparably disrupted."

He declared further: "It is an absolute falsehood on the part of the Department of Public Works to claim that

176

the affected localities asked for this expressway. It cannot provide local traffic relief unless accesses to the expressway are cut right through every village and to do that would obliterate a good part of each village. It would just about ruin Tarrytown. What the Governor has done is beyond understanding. In my opinion, the whole business is insane. It must be stopped."

In Tarrytown, a plaque in a local park has been erected on the site where Colonial militiamen apprehended the British officer, Major John André, who in 1780 was hanged as a spy for complicity in the treason of Benedict Arnold. Reference to this moment in early American history was made in a hearing by George B. Case, Chairman of the Tarrytown Planning Board and secretary of the Westchester Municipal Planning Federation. Speaking in hyperbole and anger, Mr. Case cited the case of Benedict Arnold "186 years ago."

"Then and now the man charged with the duty of defending the Hudson River attempted to betray it," he said. "Today's plot is a different twist in that the Governor, in selling out the river, would have us believe he is beautifying it. Now, as then, we need the forces of Washington to save the Hudson." Strong words, perhaps, but no stronger really than Rockefeller's designation of his opponents as "idiotic."

Though the people whose communities would be ravished by the proposed superhighways, Democrats and Republicans alike, opposed Rockefeller, one cannot say that his schemes were without support.

McMorran, not surprisingly, supported the roadways. He is, after all, not only Rockefeller's man, but also an official of several highway research and roadbuilders' organizations, whose main function is to see that more roads get built.

Edwin Michaelian, Westchester County's administrator and a Rockefeller toady, supported the highway schemes. The roads were also supported by builders, utility companies, contractors, and suppliers who would stand to gain from the project.

Part of Michaelian's political and economic power establishment is an organization called the Westchester County Association, a kind of industrial and trade society made up of representatives from 550 industries and businesses. A system prevails under which multiple memberships may be purchased. The Gannett newspapers, for example, hold numerous memberships. At important meetings, in which government and commercial delegates mingle and plan, Gannett editors are present by management command.

Offices of the Westchester County Association are located just outside the Editorial Department of the Gannett newspaper in the county seat city of White Plains, and press releases for the Association are written by the newspaper's staff in one of the more cozy public relations operations existing between a publisher and a neighboring source of news.*

The Association came out strongly in favor of the expressway and commended Governor Rockefeller for thinking of it. Then the Gannett newspapers commended the Association for taking its bold stand. The Citizens Committee for the Hudson Valley, which had been quickly formed after the expressway bill was passed, proclaimed that the endorsement of the roadway by the Westchester County Association meant primarily that contractors, sand

* The secretary of the Association, Theodore Goetz, happens also to be county newswire editor of the Westchester Gannett papers.

178

and gravel suppliers, and industries which stood to benefit by many millions of dollars in contracts were understandably eager to get started.

From the little river town of Cold Spring in the north, which is near the place called Beacon where the expressway was to originate, to Riverdale in the Bronx, citizens began importuning the President, Lady Bird Johnson, Congressmen and Senators, state legislators, New York City authorities, and each other to join in saving the Hudson shore. A heavy volume of mail, telephone calls, and telegrams flooded into Albany, all of them directed to Governor Rockefeller's deaf ear.

Assemblyman Cabot reported publicly that he and his colleagues in both the Assembly and Senate were deluged with more protests against the Hudson River Expressway Bill than the combined response to laws establishing the sales tax, ending the death sentence, and liberalizing birth control restrictions. Conservationists, newly formed citizens groups, individuals, and local public officials besieged the Governor over the issue. Cabot requested a meeting with Rockefeller, who saw him in the Executive Chamber at Albany. Cabot took with him an armload of protest mail and submitted it as evidence that the Expressway ought to be repealed.

"The Governor just glanced at the mail," said Cabot, "and listened to my report. Then he said to me, 'That's odd. I haven't heard a single objection to the expressway.' He kept a straight face, too. He added that he was determined to build the road. Mr. Rockefeller is a very arrogant fellow, indeed."

All mail and telegrams were ignored by the Governor and simply passed on to his cousin, Alexander Aldrich, who sent form answers to people saying that Governor Rockefeller "has asked me to tell you, etc."

179

As the uproar against Governor Rockefeller's expressway project mounted in the Hudson Valley, with protests ignored in Albany, and as stirrings of discontent were felt in Congress and in the White House, evidence developed as to how the Governor and J. Burch McMorran had worked together, outside the framework of government, in planning the legislative coup.

The New York Central Railroad, some months before passage of the Expressway Bill, had made available a rail bus for an unpublicized observation trip along the Central's riverfront tracks from the Bronx to an undisclosed destination up the river. The rail bus is a well-equipped and comfortable vehicle which has conventional tires for road mobility, but also has a special undercarriage set on train wheels that enable it to operate on railroad tracks.

Private engineers employed by the Rockefellers, in company with New York Central and Department of Public Works officials, made a survey trip in the rail bus and, along the way, conferred on possible site locations for the proposed expressway, how it could be aligned to avoid destruction of major industries, how it might be built on fill in shallow water at the river's edge, climb to bluffs for scenic views, come inland a few hundred feet when necessary, rise to an elevated highway over straight stretches of railroad tracks between commuter communities, and so on. The cooperation of the New York Central in this inspection tour was easily obtained, in view of the railroad's concern for maximum income from the sale of air rights over its roadbed. The railroad had acquired this supremely beautiful right-of-way in the mid-nineteenth century when the giveaway of public resources, both through legitimate purchase and unparalleled corruption, was a standard and lucrative practice. The presence of the roadbed a few yards from the river's edge prevented the development of

180

a riverfront life and the growth of marvelous waterfront communities that are commonplace along many of the river valleys and lake shores of Europe.

Still another important reason for the New York Central's interest in construction of the expressway was its long established policy of trying to get rid of, or obtain subsidies for, its commuting business. With a great highway running parallel to the railroad tracks right into New York City, a probability existed that more and more commuters might take to the road rather than the train. Any cut in commuter service income, combined with the argument that the government had further subsidized automobile travel—which it habitually does—would strengthen the case for subsidies or for curtailment of commuter runs.

No rational explanation or justification was offered for the sudden emergence of the unwanted road, or for the top secret manner in which it was privately planned outside the arena of public administration. The Governor defended the project on the grounds that for years he had been "importuned" by Hudson Valley communities to relieve local bottlenecks aggravated by through traffic, especially heavy trucking over state roads routed through the towns.

When local communities "importuned" the Governor to help relieve traffic congestion, they were not asking for a fifty-mile thruway along the riverfront which would mainly serve through traffic, half-wreck every community along the route, and still provide only marginal relief at local bottlenecks. Heavy, long-haul trucks would, of course, be removed from the local streets, but bypasses around bottleneck towns would do the same thing at a small fraction of the expressway cost—and all without ripping up the towns excessively, and especially without wiping out whatever waterfront remained or could be rehabilitated.

Some people who had held Mr. Rockefeller in high

regard when he was a Republican moderate, battling valiantly and with gusto against some very ugly political elements in the Republican Party, could not bring themselves to take part in a frontal attack on him. Many preferred to blame the Democratic majority in the State Legislature and made representations directly to the State Department of Public Works, demanding an explanation and urging the development of alternate routes. The mystique that Rockefeller, the good neighbor of the estate country, and Rockefeller the Governor were one and the same person—the conservationist, preserver of natural beauty, philanthropist, and protagonist of moderation and common sense in all things—was hard to set aside. But when public hearings on the expressway were held, evidence accumulated that whatever Nelson Rockefeller was as a member of a philanthropic family, as Governor he was a pragmatic and ruthless politician, trading off advantage for maximum power to accomplish what he personally wanted. He demanded and got acquiescence, or at least silence, within the state administration and used the leverage of his private and personal wealth to conceal both from the public and from responsible authorities knowledge of the plan to convert the bank of a great river into a traffic corridor.

The first public hearing was called by State Senator Royden A. Letsen of Yonkers, Chairman of the Senate Committee on Highways, and Assemblyman Lawrence Cabot. It was held near Tarrytown in the town hall of Greenburgh and the cost of it was paid personally by the two legislators. The hearing was boycotted by all officials of the Westchester County government, committed to stand with Nelson Rockefeller, and by all officials of the state. J. Burch McMorran announced to the press that he would not appear because "it would serve no useful purpose."

But a good number of others did appear at the hearing, waving prepared notes, breathing their rage into the hearing record in a cadence that revealed their depth of feeling. Some thirty witnesses denounced the roadway project, questioned the motive and the integrity of expressway protagonists, ridiculed the Gannett press for blatant partisanship, and pleaded for the intervention of the federal government. One witness, Robert Massie, a writer for the *Saturday Evening Post,* told the legislators that the promise of the State Department of Public Works to consult with local governments on route alignment was "utterly worthless," since, he charged, the route itself was already established by law. "Our villages and towns are being ravished," he said, "and the pledge to consult with us is the kind of consultation that occurs when a thug hauls a lady into the park and declares he is about to assault her, then offers her only the choice of park benches."

Congressman Ottinger appeared at this first local public hearing on the expressway project to announce that a subcommittee of the Interior and Insular Affairs Committee of the House of Representatives would hold a series of public hearings in the Hudson Valley. The hearings, he said, would deal with the establishment of the Hudson Highlands National Scenic Riverway under protective legislation which Ottinger had introduced in his first official act after his election.

On the hottest weekend of the summer of 1965, with the temperatures in the upper 90s, six members of the House of Representatives Subcommittee on National Parks and Recreation conducted three public hearings on the Ottinger bill (H.S. 3012) and related legislation to establish the Hudson Highlands National Scenic Riverway.

In the sweltering heat of public high school auditoriums in the Hudson River towns of Yonkers, the Tarrytowns, and the Putnam County village of Cold Spring, the hear-

183

ings were at times uproarious, exhausting—and extraordinarily revealing. The Subcommittee was joined in all of its sessions by Mr. Ottinger, who was sometimes a witness and often a guest questioner of other witnesses, and in one session by Congressman Ogden L. Reid, a Republican representing the part of Westchester outside of Ottinger's district.

From the beginning, it was obvious that the visiting Congresmen were taken aback by the fire and passion of witnesses pleading with the Subcommittee to adopt federal law to save the Hudson Valley from the kind of development encouraged and engineered by the New York State government in general, and its Governor in particular. With few exceptions, the viewpoints and evidence were polarized into intensive support or flat rejection of federal initiative to regulate, and set standards for, the explosive expansion of urban growth and conservation of natural resources in the beautiful Hudson Valley.

Nearly two hundred witnesses gave direct testimony, and sixty-one others—representing organizations, public agencies, and government bodies—submitted documentary evidence, resolutions, and correspondence. It was reported that Laurance Rockefeller would testify but he did not appear.

The Rockefeller man in Westchester, Edwin Michaelian, was scheduled to appear before the Subcommittee, but sent in his place Saul J. Prezioso, his assistant, who read Michaelian's prepared statement. The absentee county executive went right to the point, as he saw it, by suggesting that Mr. Ottinger had got the public stirred up about the Hudson River for nasty reasons.

"May I respectfully point out," read Mr. Prezioso from Michaelian's script, "that although the Hudson River was first discovered by Giovanni da Verrazano 441 years ago

184

(in 1524) and was explored by Henry Hudson 336 years ago (1609), it was only rediscovered by some last year during a congressional campaign . . .

"We recommend the abandonment of any contemplated action by the Congress to supersede the States of New York and New Jersey, our counties and our localities, as this is what we believe [the Ottinger bill] would accomplish, however well intended the purpose of its sponsors."

Congressman Leo O'Brien of New York got the floor. "The statement just read," he said, "raises a number of questions in my mind but I hesitate to ask them because, first, the gentleman who presented the statement is not here . . . But I think that while it is very nice to point out that the Hudson River was first discovered 441 years ago and explored 336 years ago, and only rediscovered during a congressional campaign, I do not think there is anyone in this room who would not concede that the Hudson River as it was 441 years ago was just a little different than the Hudson River today.

"Frankly, I am rather pleased that we did get a little injection of politics on both sides this morning because we will know which pieces of testimony to weigh most seriously." (Laughter and applause)

Joseph P. Ronan, administrative deputy from the office of J. Burch McMorran, delivered the latter's prepared statement to the Subcommittee after McMorran himself decided not to appear. Mr. Ronan seemed to have been assigned the job of appearing before local groups to sell the expressway to dissident citizens. He told the congressmen the department had "no preconceived idea of building a road on any particular location . . . and, as a matter of fact . . . if opposition to the road is so very intense, I think we probably would go elsewhere with our plan." A gasp escaped

185

the heat-wilted audience at this comment and Ottinger remarked dryly: "Very encouraging. I am glad to have that statement on the record."

The major thrust of most of the testimony protested the Con Ed power plant and the Rockefeller expressway, while at the same time calling for passage of the Ottinger bill— or something like it. Major objections denounced Congressional action as a federal take-over, denial of home rule, and intrusion into the affairs of localities.

The final hearing was held in Cold Spring on Sunday afternoon July 25, after the exhausted Congressmen, who had retired late following a reception and dinner under the larch trees at the Ottinger home in Pleasantville the preceding evening, completed a six-hour yacht trip along the river shores in the Hudson highlands.

Members of the Subcommittee, in company with a party of some twenty guests, departed on the river tour from the Peekskill Yacht Club in midmorning. A well informed guide and conservationist, Benjamin Frazier, pointed out the scenic sights and pollution outfalls as the vessel hugged the shoreline. Where waters swirling with greenish sewage entered the river at Newburgh, a young lady served luncheon.

In view of the stench and the effluence pouring into the river, the Congressmen were unable to eat the meatballs served to them. It was the most irrefutable evidence they had seen—or smelled—that the Hudson River was in dire need of restorative attention, federal or otherwise.

The six Congressmen of the Subcommittee had provided a forum unparalleled for extending the dialogue on the Hudson Valley, a forum in which legislators, local public officials, conservationists, water resource specialists, industrial executives, and citizens' groups were heard and their collective concerns publicized. The Hudson River

186

issue escaped from its regional confines and was widely reviewed in the press of the larger cities for the first time. The issue became, in fact, national instead of local, for it mirrored similar spoliation all over the country.

A few days after the congressional hearings closed, there was at long last an acknowledgment from the Governor of the intense controversy and charges that the expressway and spur would benefit primarily Rockefeller property that probably must sooner or later be developed. The Governor announced from Albany that the Rockefeller family was "extremely unhappy" over Department of Public Works plans to build a limited access Expressway through the Pocantico Hills estate. The Governor said the road "would cut the family property in two, while at the same time retaining the present route through Pocantico Hills." The latter reference was to Route 117, which the family has long hoped to close off or realign. He said the new road would go through "a beautiful section of the property which we have no intention of developing, the beauty of which would be spoiled by this new multi-lane, super commercial expressway." However, the Governor was not one to let personal interests stand in the way of necessity. He went on to say that J. Burch McMorran, his Superintendent of Public Works, "has already given a detailed statement as to why it was necessary to ask for legislative authority to build this road." "It is my duty," said Mr. Rockefeller, "to support the long range plans of the Public Works Department."

The idea that McMorran could somehow push an expressway through the Rockefeller estate over the objections of the Rockefeller family, and to the dismay of the Governor, was so preposterous as to evoke only disbelief. If Rockefeller had a duty to support his Superintendent of

Public Works, he might also have had a transcendent duty to listen to the mounting chorus of objections from his embattled constituents.

Instead, trailer offices showed up on the Rockefeller estate, offices which housed field workmen laying out the roadway route, drilling deep beneath the topsoil, plotting grade lines. On a day when it was officially announced that no route alignment had been determined, workmen were already marking off the route of the Rockefeller Spur. Rockefeller, like Con Ed at Storm King Mountain, had gone too far to stop, and had no intention of pulling back anyway.

Of the thousands of people, both in and out of scores of organizations who reacted, partly in spontaneous response and partly out of political concern, many were, of course, angered primarily by the fact that the expressway would hurt them personally—devalue their property, destroy the privacy of their homes, or bring noise, pollution, and urban sprawl to their protected sanctuaries. Concurrently, however, many of these same people were made abundantly aware that, quite aside from damage to their own private worlds, open space and riverfronts had other lasting values extending beyond their small but cherished interests. It was an education for the suburbanites, removed from the chaotic city world and isolated in their privileged affluent ghettos, to learn that what could threaten them as individuals could simultaneously threaten others. No one was safe.

An amusing sidelight in this bitter struggle came in the form of a front-page editorial in Rockefeller's home town newspaper, *The Tarrytown Daily News,* aghast at the idea that an *ad hoc* citizens committee was soliciting funds to fight the expressway. "Nothing can beat the power of money . . . Money—big money—is now at work to defeat the Hudson Expressway."

On the day the front-page battle call was sounded, the citizens' group opposing Rockefeller's roadway had $136 on hand. After some weeks, the sum was increased to $600, which was spent on newspaper ads. In eight months, the Citizens Committee for the Hudson Valley raised $8,000, all of which was spent for public relations counsel and for preparing a brief, calling for repeal of the expressway law, and distributed among legislators at Albany.

A week after the Congressional Subcommittee hearings were held in the Hudson Valley, Superintendent of Public Works J. Burch McMorran announced a new tactical ploy. He said that the state would scrap its plan to build the southernmost part of the expressway along the river from Tarrytown to the New York City line. (It is significant that a state employee was peremptorily scrapping a plan passed by the Legislature!) The reasons for the about-face, according to Mr. McMorran, were about the same ones that Governor Rockfeller's "idiotic and politically motivated" opponents had presented in the first place. It would be too costly, too destructive to property, and would not be a very good "scenic" highway anyway. It seemed there were "severe problems and disadvantages in not only constructing the new highway but in providing connections with existing highways in New York City."

Mr. McMorran said he would ask the State Legislature to rescind the law authorizing this stretch of the expressway. The remaining section of the expressway would be built, however, and would extend from Beacon in the north to a connecting access at the New York State Thruway in Tarrytown.

Laurance Rockefeller's Commission was officially cred-

189

ited with proposing elimination of part of the river road, but unofficially it was reported that the U.S. Bureau of Roads, the White House, and federal agencies were being bombarded with complaints from irate voters. The Governor's bland assertion that he hadn't received any—or, later, not very many—complaints about the road was not repeated after public hearings gave full exposure to the issue. The interest of Washington in the Hudson Valley question was fired and fed by the steady stream of objections from the Public. And from Washington, a message was getting through to Albany.

It is significant that terminating the expressway at the juncture of the Tappan Zee Thruway Bridge at Tarrytown still gave Rockefeller the expressway and east-west spur needed to enhance the future commercial values of the Rockefeller holdings.

This ploy didn't work. It was intended to divide the opposition, separating the communities still threatened and those that no longer would be. But the river towns south of Tarrytown had only the word of J. Burch McMorran that their communities had been spared. It remained an easy matter, after the election heat was off—and after the expressway was built to Tarrytown—to change policy again, as long as the expressway legislation was on the books. Citizens groups, freed of the threat of the loss of riverfront, did not give up the fight, but joined with those still faced with the project in demanding the law's repeal.

The public did not respond to the divide-and-conquer tactics, though pleased that some part of the construction was set aside. Instead, the Citizens Committee for the Hudson Valley had legal and engineering counsel prepare a ten-page critical brief calling for repeal of the expressway law and termination of the project along any and all riverfront areas. The brief was placed before every Assemblyman and

Senator in the 1966 legislature with the hope that it would evoke full repeal.

The brief set forth seven major arguments and concluded with this summary:

It is urged upon the Legislature that the subject legislation is a prime example of hasty highway planning, if it can be termed planning at all.

At a time when New York City is in the throes of a transportation crisis, it is instructive that the State Department of Public Works, without consultation either with New York City authorities or the public officials of the local communities, sought to ram through another highway without any apparent consideration of the larger aspects of planning, involving the balance between rail and road transportation.

This ill-conceived and misborn project, along with a number of other current proposals for unnecessary and damaging highway and bridge construction, points up the necessity of legislative consideration of the entire problem of highway transportation, and perhaps a moratorium on further highway construction in the metropolitan and suburban areas until a master plan can be developed to solve our current transportation problems.

As for abandonment of part of the expressway, in a pre-election response to mounting public pressure, the brief declared:

The expressway was obviously projected as a whole, and the facile abandonment of the southern half of the plan appears clearly intended to divide public opposition and secure construction of part of the expressway now and an extension south of the bridge later.

The east-west superhighway of three and a half miles, which would obliterate the countryside character of the land that has been cultivated and cared for since early Dutch manorial days, was denounced as "entirely unnecessary and of dubious purpose."

191

The citizens' brief made clear that if the State was intent on funneling even more traffic into the New York City bottlenecks, already choked beyond capacity, there was a more rational alternative. Route 9A, presently a four-lane highway, could be widened. Much of this route is over land already owned by the State. It is accessible along both sides of its corridor, which the river route would not be. The required condemnations would be at a minimum. And the estimated cost per running mile would be only $3,000,000 as opposed to the $6,000,000 to $12,000,000 for the Rockefeller-sponsored route. But the sensible alternative of Route 9A does not enhance enormously the commercial potential of the Rockefeller lands. That is why the Citizens' Committee had sadly to conclude that the Rockefeller Spur they opposed provides "at public expense future access to large land areas controlled by a single interest . . ."

Highwayman Rockefeller was triumphant.

One Man's River

8

The manipulation of power in the pursuit of personal objectives is inescapable in goverment and politics. It is quality of mind, the theme and content of one's aspirations and the application of power in the public interest—as the public interest is perceived and interpreted—that gives us the means of taking a man's measure. It is just as possible for an elected public official's actions to reflect the public interest as it is to betray it. It depends on the issue, the man, and his motives.

In seven years of on-the-job training as Governor of New York and two sustained attempts to win the Republican presidential nomination, Nelson Rockefeller addressed himself to many issues, but one question that, on the evidence, did not attract his political attention was the condition of the great Hudson River. He was not alone in this oversight since preceding governors, too, failed to initiate action to curtail or reverse the generations of abuse and ruination which afflicted the greatest river in the East and its shores.

A few days after the United States Congress began its 1965 session, Richard L. Ottinger, the young freshman representative from Rockefeller's home district, fulfilled a campaign promise to introduce a Scenic Hudson Riverway Bill. It designated the lower Hudson Valley as an area to be rehabilitated under federal jurisdiction and preserved from further ruin, if possible, by the establishment of controls under the Department of the Interior.

The Scenic Hudson bill designated a corridor extending a mile from each shore line south of Beacon as an area in which a commission, jointly named by federal and state governments, would set standards, provide public access to the river through easements, and prevent types of land usage inconsistent with the scenic, water, receational, resi- dential, and commercial resources of the valley. One provision of the law, as initially drawn, stipulated that the Federal Power Act of 1916, under which Consolidated Edison obtained its license to take over Storm King Mountain, would not be thereafter applicable in the corridor.

It was immediately clear that Rockefeller, notwithstanding the absence of any previous interest in the matter, considered the Hudson River Valley his own turf. He seemed to view the proposal of joint federal-state action as a rebuke for his own inaction and an intrusion into his own domain, apparently forgetting that the lower Hudson was New Jersey's river, too. Too late to take initiative, he saw that concern for the Hudson Valley, expressed in political terms, was giving stature and prominence to Richard Ottinger that he, Rockefeller, might have claimed. Instead, the Governor was stuck with the stigma of having tried to turn the scenic resources of the Hudson highlands over to a public utility in which his family had had a long and varied financial interest. The Governor had got on the wrong side of the Hudson issue, and now an upstart Congressman had crystallized the issue in national, as well as regional, terms. To a man like Rockefeller, it did not seem quite fair that a newcomer should be the beneficiary of so much favorable publicity and so much popular response.

194

The only defense, under the circumstances, was a strong, if belated, offense.

First, he declared that the State of New York needed no federal help or legislation to help clean up the river and arrest the blight of deterioration of the valley. Following his lead, the Gannett newspapers raised the cry that "home rule" was threatened by the Scenic Hudson bill, and charged a "federal takeover." Such fervor for local control would have seemed more sincere if the Governor or the Gannett press had not blinked the fact that the Federal Power Commission, the U.S. Army Corps of Engineers, the Atomic Energy Commission, and the U.S. Bureau of Roads had long ago involved themselves in Hudson affairs. Moreover, the proposed federal riverway bill was intended to *curb* the autonomous federal power of these agencies and make their work in the Hudson area subordinate to community interests. It was precisely the failure of the local communities and the state to apply or enforce *any* rules that had led, finally, to Ottinger's bill.

Nelson Rockefeller's response was characteristic and quick. It called for keeping the focus of retaliatory action in the family and organizing political associates, friends, and colleagues into a study commission which could be counted on to subordinate itself to the Governor's views.

He named his brother Laurance, already chairman of the State Council on Parks, head of a new agency called the Hudson River Valley Commission and directed the Commission to "formulate recommendations" for improving conditions along the river, setting aside recreational sites, parks, and so on, and to make a report to the 1966 session of the State Legislature. The elderly and affable Conrad L. Wirth, for many years Director of the National Parks Service in the U.S. Department of the Interior, was engaged as executive director of the Commission and set up in new offices in the Rockefeller Plaza in New York City.

Neither Mr. Wirth nor William H. Whyte, a conservationist author-member of the Governor's Commission, had to relocate since both were employed by the American Conservation Association, which had the same offices and telephone numbers as brother Laurance Rockefeller.

In addition to the Commission members themselves, the Governor appointed thirty-seven people to serve on the Advisory Committee to the Hudson River Valley Commission. The Advisory Committee was a top-heavy collection of some of the last people in the world one might recruit to offer counsel on the fate and future of the Hudson River and its environs. His selections included:

L. A. Tobey, works manager of the U.S. Gypsum Company, one of the industrial operations which has used the Hudson as a sewer.

Charles L. Hulswit, president of Orange & Rockland Utilities, Inc., Nyack, New York, producer of power.

Edward F. Cavanagh, Jr., then deputy mayor of New York and brother-in-law of Mayor Robert F. Wagner.

Charles E. Eble, lobbyist extraordinary, president of the Consolidated Edison Company, and previously well-rewarded friend of Governor Rockefeller.

Joseph H. Green, manager of the North Tarrytown Chevrolet plant of General Motors Corporation—polluter of the Hudson River, and one of the three largest taxpayers in Rockefeller estate territory.

Thomas V. Kennedy, vice president of Poirier and McLane Corporation in Yonkers, New York, an engineering and building firm which has done a great deal of work in Westchester and which Lieutenant Governor Malcolm Wilson's law firm has represented in the past.

Alfred E. Perlman, president of the New York Central Railroad, whose main line tracks run along the eastern bank of the river all the way to Albany, making the river all but inaccessible much of the way.

Lelan F. Sillin, Jr., president of the Central Hudson Gas and Electric Corporation, which wants to build its own hydroelectric plant along the river.

Holt Winfield, manager of industrial relations for the Kay-Friese Chemical Company at West Haverstraw, New York, one of many chemical plants dumping waste into the Hudson.

Edwin G. Michaelian, Rockefeller's Westchester man.

Not all thirty-seven members of the advisory group had direct conflicts of interest that obviously stood in the way of any objective counsel they might give. Some of the appointees simply had not concerned themselves especially about the Hudson Valley's problem, but welcomed their appointments as an opportunity to learn something about it. Thus their counsel could be expected to have a quality of freshness, uncorrupted from having studied the matter excessively.

Still others seemed to be qualified primarily because of their prior commitment to Governor Rockefeller's position, or at best a readiness to adapt to it. One of these was Dr. Harold G. Wilm, then Commissioner of the New York State Conservation Department, who had described the mass destruction of fish at Con Edison's Indian Point nuclear power plant as "an act of God" which could not be prosecuted at the earthly or river level.

Another was Keith S. McHugh, former president of the New York Telephone Company, a highly able man who was appointed Commissioner of the New York State Department of Commerce by Rockefeller.

Finally, there was William J. Cannon, an editorial

writer on one of the Gannett newspapers, the *Tarrytown Daily News.* Mr. Cannon is something of a character in the circulation area of the *Daily News,* where his editorials, while unsigned, are instantly recognizable by their circumspect, and at times incomprehensible, prose and by the uncompromising dismissal of all points of view which fail to mesh with Rockefeller's. He is quite old now, but remains an aggressive, unquestioning, and militant supporter of Nelson and all his works.

Any lingering hope of conservationist friends of Governor Rockefeller that he was seriously determined to rehabilitate the Hudson River and perhaps reclaim it as a great natural resource area diminished with publication of the names of thirty-seven people he selected to lay down guidelines for study and action.

Further evidence that Rockefeller was not really selecting personnel to guard the state's natural resources was made painfully clear when he announced his choice for a successor to the departed Dr. Wilm, who had vacated the state's top post in the Department of Conservation. He is R. Stewart Kilborne of Katonah in Westchester County, a man with absolutely no perceptible qualifications or background in conservation, or the field of natural resources management. The press release announcing the appointment went to some pains to point out that he was an ardent hunter and fisherman who trekked the Adirondacks for game and went to New Brunswick for salmon. The job pays Mr. Kilborne $30,000 a year. Robert Boyle, an editor of *Sports Illustrated* magazine and a leading authority on wildlife and conservation, when informed of Governor Rockefeller's choice of a new Conservation Commissioner, could only ask wearily, "Who's he?"

Upon reflection, it was recognized that even people of obvious qualifications for the post, as Dr. Harold Wilm had been when he took the position in 1959, are hopelessly disabled if the first criterion of job measurement is total subordination to Governor Rockefeller. It is perhaps just as well that a Westchester Republican fund raiser take over the job, since there is less chance that he might have to violate his philosophical and professional credentials. If the appointment of a Michaelian crony to the top jurisdictional post over state resources, coupled with the roster of Hudson River commission advisors, was intended to show contempt for informed and professional judgment arrayed against Rockefeller, it was successful.

With the River Commission and its advisory staff established, the Governor was obliged to get it functioning. Since he shared control of the Legislature with Mayor Robert Wagner, he was able to slip the Hudson River Expressway and the Rockefeller Spur into law, free of any objections from the commission, which was carefully kept in ignorance.

With this detail out of the way, Mr. Rockefeller extracted from the nondeliberative Legislature something called the New York State Scenic Hudson Corridor Bill. It gave to Laurance Rockefeller and the River Commission $270,000 to make studies and come up with recommendations. Second, it defined the Corridor as all the land a mile back from both sides of the Hudson for its *entire length,* from the New York harbor to its northernmost reaches upstate. If Rockefeller was going to preserve the Hudson River, by gad, he was going all the way. The bill was not debated, analyzed, or studied. It was just introduced and passed.

This hastily drafted piece of legislation, Rockefeller's retaliation against federal proposals backed by thirty-nine Senators and Representatives of the U.S. Congress, was meaningless in the important sense that no state law has any bearing on the power of federal agencies to com-

199

mandeer both public and private property anywhere. People bewildered by the grandiose scheme needn't have been especially concerned. As it developed, Nelson Rockefeller was never serious about the unenforceable proposals anyway.

Long before the state's grandstand river bill was signed by the Governor, Laurance Rockefeller discussed federal proposals with Secretary of the Interior Stewart Udall, and was assured that New York State could plan its own river rehabilitation programs before Congress was likely to review the matter. Udall and Laurance are old friends in the conservation business, so an arrangement between them was not surprising. However, while Udall was standing by, giving New York State time to study the matter, Governor Rockefeller and J. Burch McMorran had the Hudson River Expressway law passed, without consulting anybody. Udall did not feel that putting a superhighway along the Hudson contributed much to the river's future. He was pretty disenchanted with the Governor.

Regardless of his chilled feelings, he waited with other interested parties until Laurance Rockefeller's Hudson River Commission came up with its report to the Legislature in 1966. When finally published, the Hudson River Commission report contained a candid statement almost identical to the criticism previously directed against the State government and the Federal Power Commission:

"There has been an appalling lack of joint effort to anticipate the opportunities. So far, few of the individual projects seem planned in relation to one another, and in far too many instances they [are] planned for a single purpose."

This read like a long-awaited condemnation of the riverfront expressway, which hadn't been planned at all and certainly was not a "joint effort."

Yet, Laurance's Commission approved brother Nelson's

200

road construction project, thereby giving support to the kind of planning it denounced as "appalling." Things were back to normal.

The Commission did suggest that Consolidated Edison ought to look for an alternative site for its hydroelectric plant and recommended acquisition of Storm King for a state park—a remarkable change of fate for that embattled mountain. Also proposed:

• Acquisition of 150 specific areas totaling 100,000 acres to provide "a coherent system of usable open spaces," with money to be provided from a Hudson River Fund of $100 million—half to be provided by the Federal Government and the other half by State and private sources.

• Passage by referendum of a $200 million New York State Recreation bond issue, to be used in part to reclaim certain areas sealing off access to, "and even sight of," the river.

• A system of privately owned marinas.

• A linear, or "noodle-shaped," park thirty-two miles in length and sixty-six feet wide, along the site of the 130-year-old Croton Aqueduct, which carried water from reservoirs in upper Westchester County to New York City. This would be a hiking and cycling trail—a kind of public walkway.

• Control and elimination of junk yards and billboards in scenic river areas, to improve the view of the land from the river.

• Wayside areas, complete with parking places and restrooms, "to take advantage of natural features such as streams, scenic lookouts, and wooded areas."

• A Hudson River motor tourway, a network using existing roadways and the river to connect the "cultural, historic and scenic resources of the valley"; also, special identifying markers and trained guides.

• Protection of nonpublicly owned land by selective

purchase and use of easements, and to make such lands accessible for hiking and riding trails, canoe routes, and campsites.

• Encouragement of riverfront urban renewal programs to provide more marinas, shoreside motels, pedestrian shopping malls, promenades, and restaurants looking out on the water. "Each of the old riverfront cities has something comparable to a fisherman's wharf, and as other shoreside cities have discovered, these can be made into a great drawing card."

• Use of the underside of bridges to carry utility lines across the river.

• Curtailment and regulation of riverfront quarry sites, with relocation inland where possible.

• Harbor cleanup and removal of debris to aid navigation.

• Enforcement of the law prohibiting sewage discharge from river craft.

• Establishment of a compact between the Federal Government, New Jersey, and New York for future planning in the Hudson Valley. "The commission would not be a supergovernment. It would work primarily through existing agencies and local governments . . . to guide the over-all planning efforts and to help governments and private groups. . . ."

The commission would have "authority to review plans for government-aided projects which would have substantial effect on the valley. The commission would also review applications for government licenses for major private projects, such as the construction of utility plants. . . . The commission would not have veto power [but] if it felt a project wrong . . . an adverse report could have very considerable influence."

Governor Rockefeller asked Governor Hughes of New

Jersey and the appropriate Federal authorities to move at once to form the three-entity compact, which also requires New York State legislation.

The report of the Hudson River Commission clearly indicated that the state, with some of Laurance Rockefeller's views gaining ascendancy, had filed a strong claim on jurisdictional rights for regulating the reclamation and development of the Hudson Valley. Laurance, who holds dozens of posts in the conservation and philanthropic fields, is one of the nation's great figures in the preservation and ecological rehabilitation of land, water, and resources.

Yet, the concentration and intermingling of family, personal, economic, and governmental power in the conservation field is worrisome to some people, even those whose enterprises and public service programs benefit by Laurance's vast knowledge, great good will, and welcome contributions of money. One such worried person is a high-ranking conservationist expert working with foundations, wealthy families, and government agencies.

"I am troubled," he said, "by the overlapping of public and private interests at times. The problem is, when a foundation has a good idea or a long-range project in the field of conservation, or in saving some valuable resource for the future, Laurance is always there. He takes the time, the interest, and the money to get things done or help you get them done.

"He is an expert ecologist, although that is not his profession. He is above criticism on nearly all counts, I would say, but he and Nelson Rockefeller, their competent professional staffs, and their extensive influence raise in my mind a question of excessive, if benevolent, authority.

"The Con Ed plant, the Hudson River superhighway, that bridge of Robert Moses's across Long Island Sound— you don't know whether they are necessary, or whether

203

alternatives would offer reasonably similar solutions at less cost, less disruption to human beings, and more sense in the long run.

"The fact is, nobody puts all the values together, compares the alternatives, and comes to a decision in which all the values receive the consideration they merit.

"We must develop in this country some kind of an Office of Strategic Planning that puts indispensable needs of the future, and the whole human scale, into a rational perspective. It is utterly senseless to have people and agencies, working more or less in secret, independently developing ideas which, when formulated, are practically imposed without review.

"I worry about conservation organizations being silenced in their support or opposition to things because the Rockefellers or the Mellons may favor or oppose their planning. The mere presence of this kind of power, which has one foot in government and the other in vast private fortunes, makes for lack of clarity.

"Then, too, power tends to gravitate to power. Last year, four important parks and recreation organizations merged into one and Laurance moved in as titular head of the amalgamated organization.

"This country is deeply indebted to the benevolence I speak of, and Laurance Rockefeller is one of the best men in the world in his field, but we are working for the future and the public. When it comes to manipulating irreplaceable values, I wish we were on surer ground."

In the light of all the study, planning, and money that went into the long-awaited report of Rockefeller's Hudson River Commission, it was incomprehensible that no law was recommended to enforce the provisions or reclamation projects proposed. The commission did no more than suggest the power of persuasion as an alternative to enforce-able legislation. Only "an adverse report" might be issued against offenders.

The naïve idea that Consolidated Edison, Governor Rockefeller, or the Federal Power Commission would desist in the face of "an adverse report" was an expression of faith that could move mountains, Storm King or otherwise. The power of persuasion had taken a drubbing for a hundred years in the Hudson Valley and was not growing any stronger.

One of the more startling proposals in the report was the recommendation that Governor Rockefeller would appoint nine of the fifteen members to carry out the pro-posals of the compact between New Jersey, New York, and the Federal government. The main functions of the Federal government and New Jersey would be to appoint three members each, put up money, make suggestions, and retire quietly among the perpetuated minority. There was not much of a chance for any combination of outsiders to fool around with Nelson Rockefeller's river.

As welcome as some of the Commission's recommenda-tions were, in view of their acknowledgment of the prob-lems, there was no likelihood of any concrete, enforceable program going forward unless new law—the kind of law Nelson didn't want—backed them up.

Nevertheless, the idea of New York and New Jersey joining with the Federal Government in the protection and rehabilitation of the Hudson River Valley was an accept-able one, or so it seemed, to all the participants. With this understood, in March of 1966 forty-one Senators and Representatives in Congress supported a bill in Congress to give the Secretary of Interior veto powers for three years over all federal actions in the Hudson Valley. It didn't cur-tail any specific state actions, just federal. The idea of the bill was to give the two states and federal agencies time to work out the three-government compact and to make the Hudson River Commission's recommendations applicable. It had the backing of Governor Hughes and Senator Harrison Williams of New Jersey, Secretary Udall, Senator Robert Kennedy, Congressman Ottinger, and many, many others in both parties from many states. They all thought they were helping Governor Rockefeller achieve what he *said* he wanted.

They were all wrong. Some were bewildered and others were shocked by the Governor's next move.

Ottinger, after publicly commending Governor Rockefeller for devising the three-government compact, called on him in New York. At the very moment the Congressman and the Governor were conferring on the Hudson Valley matter, a strong letter from Mr. Rockefeller was in the hands of President Johnson. The letter denounced the bill, which Ottinger, Governor Hughes, and others had thought provided interim stability during which the Rockefeller program could be studied and advanced. Rockefeller had asked the President to stop passage of the bill. He wanted no federal assistance, no intervention, no help. Most of all, he wanted no delays of his own pet projects. It became abundantly clear that he was far less interested in the great Hudson Valley program for the future than he was in his immediate impulsively contrived roadbuilding projects along the river and across his own estate.

No accommodation with Rockefeller seemed possible. He would tolerate no interference from the federal government, or local governments within the state, or the people who elected him. He would run things his way in the state and—if his plans succeeded—perhaps in the country, too.

The Three-dimensional Billionaire

Because power in government and politics gravitates to the top, there is room around the high ruling plateau for very few people. From the infinite bottom and the pyramidal middle, men of energy, ambition, and sometimes even idealism work their way toward the summit where the opportunities, dangers, and rewards are.

Nelson Rockefeller has differed from most aspirants to public office. Like a favored suitor who married into the upper echelon of the corporation, he had both money and impeccable attributes, was strong on management and administration, but was not well grounded in the territory. He went in at the top and, up to now, has stayed there, untoppled by competitors seeking to displace him, but unable to get full command of the party management.

He is, in effect, exactly where he started, Governor of the State of New York, the only job for which he was ever elected, and the only one, it appears—with the exception of the presidency—he wants. But in order to keep open the line of advance, along which the hope of personal progress lies, it is essential for him to remain where he is. To cling to a territory, fight off the attackers, keep the fences secure around the stockade—these are the necessary defensive tactics of politics, especially when the pursuers are nearing the gates.

207

The political career of Nelson Rockefeller approached another critical stage in 1966, a crucial year also for New York's politically independent John Lindsay, whose flight to the future seemed set on a collision course with the baron of Pocantico Hills. Neither Lindsay nor Rockefeller arranged matters this way but, as in the case of the famed nonprofit corporation which achieved its status unintentionally, that's how things turned out.

Nobody like John Lindsay has showed up in American city politics for many years. A highly regarded ex-Congressman representing the polyglot Silk Stocking district of Manhattan, Lindsay was young, athletic, and possessed a heroic physical constitution that promised to sustain him through the job of being Mayor of the municipal monster that is New York. He went into office virtually as a nonpartisan, or all-party, candidate, taking on and defeating old guard power blocs that seemed as securely entrenched as the Mormons in Utah.

Submerging his Republican Party affiliations to the point of invisibility, Lindsay led a fusion ticket, the first put together since Fiorello LaGuardia conducted a lively salvage operation on the city a generation ago. To the chagrin, if not the horror, of the uprooted old Democratic-Labor coalitions of New York City, the Negro and Puerto Rican communities renounced their old habit of voting for *any* Democrat and made Lindsay Mayor. It was an astounding personal victory. Everyone else on Lindsay's ticket was beaten by party line Democrats. Lindsay's new associates were not disposed to help him topple an old, moribund power establishment in favor of any new program to revive the crippled metropolis if that meant helping Lindsay as a political figure.

One of the unwelcome associates elected to serve the Lindsay Administration was a former District Attorney, smooth-talking, Celtic-handsome Frank D. O'Connor, the new President of the New York City Council who wants to be, in due course, the Governor of New York.

A wary Rockefeller, with a hungry eye on the large New York City vote, offered both assistance and money to help Lindsay throw the Democratic power brokers out of the temple in the mayoralty campaign, but Lindsay held him off. Since there seemed to be a good deal of public disenchantment with Rockefeller at the time, any close association with the Governor was felt to be more negative than helpful. Rockefeller's political marriage with Mayor Wagner in the sales tax deal, plus his connections with some of the subcults in the city's unsavory old power structure, would have tarnished the image of the fresh, professional new administration Lindsay had in mind.

Lindsay's rebuff of Rockefeller, while essential to the former's election, may cost him dearly. The Governor and his Republican following joined the Democrats, both in New York City and Albany, to prevent the Mayor from achieving fiscal and administrative reforms which Lindsay promised in his campaign and which he declared were crucial to the city's operations. Much of the 1966 session of the State Legislature was devoted to deciding whether, and how, to clobber Lindsay into political ruin, to provide minimal legislative cooperation that might offer the city no help while *appearing* to help, or whether or not to legislate the taxes and reforms Lindsay is committed to establish.

One of the pleasures of politics is observing the misery of others, especially among contenders for high office. Rockefeller could not permit the emergence of John Lindsay as a Republican competitor for the presidential nomination. With nearly every major city in the country in serious trouble, Lindsay would certainly attract national Republican attention if his administration could demonstrate both a vote-getting record in an urban populace while at the same time effectively coming to grips with problems of transportation, traffic, fiscal needs, housing, racial strife, and so on. Rockefeller was more likely to enjoy Lindsay failures, if they could be arranged, than successes. This, of course, is normal in the politics of both parties, as Lyndon Johnson's tactics against Robert Kennedy attest. Rockefeller was in an ideal position to prevent Lindsay from successfully coping with the horrendous problems of the city.

In fact, Rockefeller could count on a bipartisan coalition to help demolish Lindsay. The old power brokers of the Democratic Party in New York who had, with a large assist from the Governor, brought the city to its deplorable plight, were joined by President Johnson in the pleasant exercise of ganging up on the fusion administration of John Lindsay.

When the new Mayor entered office in January of 1966, the city was paralyzed by a transit strike that, as a legacy from the Wagner administration, had been brewing for months. While the disaster focused national attention on Lindsay for two weeks, the strike was ultimately settled with thorough illegality. It was illegal because a twenty-year-old state law, the Condon-Wadlin Act, made it so, and illegal because the city was forbidden by law to pay wage increases that were a condition of the settlement. Governor Rockefeller and the State Legislature obliged the law-breakers by hurriedly passing a law absolving the 35,000 transit workers from punishment and giving ex post facto sanction to the $75 million in wage increases they won.

President Johnson, worried about inflation, rebuked Lindsay for the strike settlement, on the grounds that the wage increases were excessive. Johnson himself was rebuked in the press for yielding to an irresistible opportunity to humiliate the Republican-fusion Mayor and doing his bit to help wreck a promising, if already threatened, political career.

With strong alliances in both major political parties directing fire at Lindsay, Rockefeller faced up to the job of running again. In the Legislature, Rockefeller scrambled to pass the new minimum wage of $1.50 an hour into law, a law which he had said a year earlier would drive business out of New York State. He scrambled just as fast to get the Condon-Wadlin Act repealed, after refusing either amendments or repeal for nearly eight years.

Building a vote-getting record was hampered somewhat by the outbreak of yet another scandal. Legislative discourse in Albany disclosed that a couple of legislators had collected housing construction fees—$27,633 in one case, $666,667 in another—under a law they had personally proposed, with the Governor's approval. Mr. Rockefeller tried as hard as he could to let that one slide by unnoticed, at least by him.

At one time, Governor Rockefeller demonstrated extraordinary administrative ability in government. In his early legislative experience, he took command of a cooperative body of lawmakers and drove through revenue-producing measures which previous administrations, both Democratic and Republican, were too timid or inept to undertake. With counsel and help from nearly fifty privately assembled task forces, he investigated and analyzed every department and service under state jurisdiction and, in a relatively short time, assimilated encyclopedic knowledge of governmental affairs. Thus authoritatively informed, he could propose and dispose with professional competence. This administrative know-how, unlike his judgment and even motives, has seldom been questioned. He expanded state services and helped feed back to hard-pressed communities substantial funds which bold, unpopular new tax policies produced. Even so, he offered himself as presidential timber from New York, a state that remains far down the list—thirty-fifth in the nation—in the percentage of revenues shared with local governments. Pragmatists might argue that this is about all an electorate, too often unconcerned anyway, can expect, and that Rockefeller is a better elected servant than most.

But government measured in such terms is corporate storekeeping. It is the kind of government that takes pride in a state fiscal policy which allows selective profiteering outside the legal requirements of bond issues and budgeting;

And which keeps the budgetmaking process secret, conducted "in a bank vault, not in a goldfish bowl," as an Albany correspondent wrote, thus keeping from public knowledge the alternatives to both the amounts and often the reasons for funds expended;

Which rations essential information, and even withholds it entirely, for the purpose of separating the people from the decision-making process;

Which allows a great but endangered American city like New York to use the Legislature to legalize one of the most unwarranted and reckless revenue-raising programs ever devised (the so-called borrow-now, legalize-it-later-by-referendum plan);

Which assists in bringing about the near fiscal ruin of America's greatest city, then all but abdicates its responsibility for helping to repair the ensuing damage;

Which fails to comply with its own laws on the care and education of the mentally retarded in its own institutions, possibly because they have no lobby;

Which deceives its constituent towns and villages by authorizing, virtually in secret and surely without consent,

212

an expressway violating all planning concepts—and which only the Governor and the roadbuilders wanted;

Which countenances profiteering, corruption, and unethical conduct with public indifference and silence on the part of the elected Chief Executive;

Which offers discriminatory and favorable treatment to law violators if they are united in sufficient numbers to make the treatment politically profitable;

Which responds to a criminal liquor scandal, involving the Governor's associates, with procedures and a new law that contradicts the results promised;

Which pledges fiscal stability, in a transparent and pandering deception, to an electorate whose taxes it then raises;

Which levies a sales tax against the people when less injurious alternatives, more humane to the poor and disadvantaged, are clearly available;

Which confers its power and support on an antipublic utility, bent on occupying scenic lands that are a national treasure—again when alternatives are clearly available;

Which hastily devises a plan to rehabilitate and restore the blighted Hudson Valley, without intention of seeking law to do so, as an act of retaliation against a threat of more effective action by others;

Which confers upon its Governor and his family corporation tax benefits and, just possibly, certain exemptions from sales taxes inflicted upon the rest of the state;

Which capriciously ignores or enforces an old labor law (the Condon-Wadlin Act), depending upon the political power of the offending unions;

Which withholds amended minimum-wage legislation until an election year for the transparent purpose of attracting the support of the poor and underpaid in a gubernatorial election;

213

Which quietly allocates many millions of dollars in public funds to build an unwanted and unneeded express highway across the Rockefeller family estate.

During Nelson Rockefeller's eight years as Governor, a complaisant Legislature has been generous with funds, with the state budget rising from $2 billion to $4 billion in two Rockefeller terms, not counting hundreds of millions of dollars committed outside of the state budget.

Yet, even with substantial gains in the development of the State's educational program, affluent New York lags, by any standard of measurement, behind less endowed states in terms of both quality of education and percentage of population receiving educational opportunity.

In nearly eight years of Nelson Rockefeller's life as an elected public official, his public image has altered from that of a dynamic, creative, and evocative political leader to a somewhat jaded, tricky, and defensive manipulator struggling for a political future.

There is no presumption, and indeed sympathy prevents the presumption, that Rockefeller's failure has been his alone. Exposure in politics is a wearying, disenchanting process at best and a man's achievements, his frailties and follies in an arena where popularity and competitive warfare meet in head-on conflict, are not always understood or appreciated. Winston Churchill, Adlai Stevenson, Thomas E. Dewey, Richard Nixon, and Nelson Rockefeller, among thousands of others, have had to brood upon this unpleasant fact.

But Mr. Rockefeller has taken the initiative in exposing his own deficiencies. Confidence imposed upon him by a hopeful electorate could not be expected to obtain in the Coliseum of reality. Yet there is a ring of continuing truth in Walter Lippman's view that Mr. Rockefeller looked down upon the people. He has surrounded himself with experts and imagemakers, subordinates and sycophants at times, who upon measurement do not appear to be experts so much as associates in a corporate enterprise.

The assumption that commercial, corporate, or philanthropic virtues are easily convertible to government is an American fallacy. Government leadership in its best forms requires an appreciation of and a response to human values.

Charles Wilson, former president of General Motors and Secretary of Defense under Dwight D. Eisenhower, disclosed an unfamiliarity with these sensibilities and values in a single, salty statement: "What's good for General Motors is good for the country." He had overtly confused the public interest with a vested corporate interest and while he didn't appear to know it, millions of others did. It's true that when General Motors prospers, the economic health of the rest of the country is also good. But the point Mr. Wilson ignored was that there is no necessary correspondence between the effect of individual actions affecting General Motors and the rest of us. This is the point that Nelson Rockefeller misses also. What's good for the Rockefellers is not necessarily good for everybody else, and in a democracy people quite properly think the final vote rests with them.

Mr. Rockefeller is said, especially in reports and literature bearing his *imprimatur,* to genuinely like people. He has a sunny disposition, especially at campaign time, that indicates a love of nonideological combat. Yet, in a conceptual conflict which puts the rampant roadbuilders and Consolidated Edison on one side, with a vast nonpartisan body of people, motivated by impersonal but important concerns, on the other, his choice is offensive to the people.

215

Moreover, his contempt for opposition shows, as when he described so many of his constituents as "idiotic and politically motivated."

This contradiction reflects a widely known condition of corporate public relations, in which a pretentious publicity program will often support the public interest while serving as a disarming shield behind which to pursue a vested, profiteering course. Happy exceptions exist to this generalization, to be sure, just as there is an occasional producer of electric power which puts lines underground and educates the public to accept safe, silent nuclear plants in urban areas rather than commandeer a scenic mountain.

Economic life and competition being what they are, it is perhaps understandable for corporate enterprises to pretend to an idealism which must be violated in the pursuit of profit. But in the case of Nelson Rockefeller, his lack of responsiveness to public need, indeed his selfishness, seems to be without purpose. Of what conceivable use to him is economic gain? What, then, are the motives for his self-delusions? You do not beautify a mountain by putting a power plant on it, or a riverfront by building a great expressway on it.

It is essential for a government, or a Governor, at times to take positions and actions that are unpopular. An electorate responds to them begrudgingly or with yielding resistance when their essentiality can be demonstrated. Leadership must inform, enlighten, and truthfully explain.

In administering the affairs of government, Nelson Rockefeller has demonstrated experience, range, and extraordinary ability. But many times his reasoning for expressed positions has been deceptive and his judgment faulty—so much so that he has had to abandon his positions, reverse them, or rerationalize them.

To learn through error is both human and useful. But

to err in arrogance, to be silent for safety's sake when issues need a voice, to become overcommitted in the face of reasonable alternative courses—and contrary to measurable evidence—gives the electorate cause for concern.

Nelson Rockefeller began at the top, entered political life as Governor of New York, known by name and charged with dynamism, but sheltered behind the walls of enormous wealth, a billionaire with an inherited social conscience, protected, certain that his will and the public's should be the same.

The last eight years have shown that, with all his energy, his personal courage, his manipulative and management abilities, he is a man of considerable skill, deeply flawed by the compulsion to have his own way.

Of course, the electorate itself is flawed, too. Voters can be greedy, stupid, indifferent, cynical, apathetic, cowardly, and prejudiced, and also intelligent, courageous, concerned, and honorable.

They can elect him Governor again. Or President.

Index

220

221

222